"I have been surprised at the intensity with which some of my colleagues have defended their belief that an anxiety state is due either to some deep-seated cause (perhaps subconscious) or to some character inadequacy and that the illness can be cured only if such causes are found and treated. As already pointed out, sensitization can come to anyone at any time, and to be bewildered by its acute and baffling symptoms is surely not unnatural. It is difficult to understand why the many people who respond in this natural way should be automatically thought inadequate or why finding some deep seated cause thought essential."

Claire Weekes, M.D.- *Agoraphobia*

Best wishes!

WHEN ANXIETY ATTACKS

WHAT THE HEALTH CARE COMMUNITY DOES NOT KNOW ABOUT ANXIETY

Stan H. Looper, M.A. and Cynthia M. Scott, M.S.

SWAN PUBLISHERS

New York * Texas * California

Library of Congress Catalog Number 93-085199
ISBN 0-943629-08-X

The names and identifying details of individual case histories presented in this book have been changed to protect their privacy.

WHEN ANXIETY ATTACKS is available in quantity discounts. Please address to: SWAN Publishing, 126 Live Oak, Suite 100, Alvin, TX 77511 (713) 388-2547 or FAX (713) 585-3738

Printed in the United States of America

Dedication

We dedicate this book to all those who suffer from high levels of anxiety, anxiety attacks, or any one of the hundreds of common phobias.

Editors: Pete Billac and Sharon Davis
Cover: Glen Clark
Publisher: SWAN Publishing Company

CONTENTS

Preface

Anxiety attacks have long been seen as a "brain disease" treated most effectively with medications, or the result of a "hidden trauma" cured with insight therapy, or as a pattern of "irrational thoughts" treated best with cognitive therapy. We have found, through our treatment of clients with anxiety attacks, that these views do not address the true causes of anxiety and therefore are not effective in eliminating the result of it...anxiety attacks.

At our Center for Phobias and Panic Attacks, we have made some exciting discoveries concerning the treatment of anxiety attacks. We have found that successful treatment for eliminating anxiety attacks can be practical and brief, usually lasting three weeks to three months.

As advocates for individuals who suffer with anxiety attacks we believe that for therapists to successfully treat this disorder, they should change the way they view the "helping process." After 10 years of specializing in the treatment of anxiety attacks we have developed a more practical therapy for our clients.

The traditional method of psychotherapy (working with clients in the office) is an approach that works well with depression and other psychological disorders but is not an effective approach for anxiety disorders such as anxiety attacks. Using the same "hammer" for all psychological problems simply does not work.

For therapists to have the same success with these types of disorders, a more flexible approach is necessary. We label this treatment "field work." We recommend that therapists leave their offices and conduct therapy where the problem occurs. If it's in someone's home, on the elevator, in the grocery store, or driving down a crowded freeway, it is pertinent to success to help them where the problem occurs.

If you are a person who has anxiety attacks and need professional help, we urge you to find a therapist who will do "field work" with you. If you are a health care professional, we urge you to work "in the field" with your clients rather than try to instruct them from your office. Your understanding of their problem will be greatly enhanced and the rewards of brief and successful treatment will be worth it.

This text will explain our more "practical" therapy for anxiety and, hopefully, serve as a guide for you to better understand how anxiety attacks develop, what causes them to escalate, and how to treat them.

Stan H. Looper, M.A. and Cynthia M. Scott, M.S.

Introduction

WHAT THE HEALTH CARE COMMUNITY DOES NOT KNOW ABOUT ANXIETY

". . . It has been estimated that the average patient, newly diagnosed with panic disorder, had seen 10 physicians before obtaining the diagnosis."

". . . In a series of patients who were referred for a coronary angiography and turned out to have normal coronary arteries, 43 percent had panic disorder. Another study found that among patients who were referred for coronary evaluation and found normal on several tests of heart function, 58 percent had panic disorder."

". . . A group survey of panic disorder patients found that they, on the average, made 37.3 medical visits a year as compared to about 5 a year for the general population."

National Institute of Mental Health

DO THESE STATISTICS ALARM YOU? More than three million Americans have anxiety attacks. These are the "*known*" numbers, but as these quotes suggest, the actual figures are probably much higher. What does this mean for you? It means that if you have repeated physical symptoms such as numbness in your hands or feet, a racing heartbeat or palpitations, dizziness or light headedness, smothering sensations, trembling hands, choking, hot flashes, profuse sweating, persistent diarrhea or "queasy" stomach around certain situations, fears of dying, losing control or going crazy, and are being treated for a physical or emotional problem other than anxiety disorders, you may be one of the *"casualties"* of a system that nine out of ten times, misdiagnoses and mistreats anxiety and panic disorders.

Many of you will label these symptoms as an *"anxiety attack."* Clinically, if you have at least four of the symptoms more than once in any four week period, you would be diagnosed as having a *"panic disorder."* For purposes of familiarity for our reader, and to emphasis the cause of the disorder, we will use the more common term, *"anxiety attack"* for these symptoms.

* * *

In 1978, I graduated from a progressive program for the study of counseling psychology. Being an honors graduate, I was sure I had learned everything necessary to help me guide my future clients with any psychological problem they might have. I learned to do *insight therapy* and *cognitive behavioral therapy.* I was taught that nearly all psychological disorders were the result of either irrational thoughts or of chemical imbalances in the brain.

Later, I realized I was taught everything there was to know about the treatment of depression but *very little* about anxiety treatment. When I graduated, I had never heard the terms *"anxiety attack"* or *"panic attack."* Anxiety disorders were never a focus and we never studied the condition "agoraphobia" (the fear of leaving home alone).

After graduation, I worked as a counselor for several different mental health agencies and then at a university for six years. In the years I worked for the university, I knew what was being taught in the current counseling classes. It was basically the same: insight therapy, cognitive therapy, medication treatment, and a class in behavioral therapy addressing classroom behavior, and snake and dog phobias.

The basic focus was still on how to treat depression. The assumption was that the primary treatment tools for depression (insight and cognitive therapy) could be effectively applied to any psychological problem. Anxiety disorders were rarely, if ever, addressed.

It has been our experience that the majority of people seeking treatment for anxiety attacks receive depression treatment instead. It is the premise of this book that the treatments for anxiety and the treatment for depression are very different and cannot be used interchangeably.

Getting depression treatment for your anxiety is similar to having the accelerator stuck in your car and having someone try to fix it by changing the oil. You can change the oil a hundred times and it will not unstick your accelerator. This is the same as going to "*insight*" therapy, "*expressive*" therapy, or "*cognitive*" therapy - all successful tools in the treatment of depression - but they will not lower your general anxiety level or stop your anxiety attacks.

For most people who have anxiety attacks, medication (*Valium, Xanax, Klonopin, Imipramine, Prozac, MAO Inhibitors, etc.)* only creates more problems. The list of common problems related to medication includes emotional or chemical dependency, over sedation and extreme preoccupation with "*side effects*", rendering the benefits of any relief from anxiety questionable. Yet, there is an extreme reluctance by physicians, psychiatrists and psychotherapists to look at this ineffectiveness. Those of you who are involved in these treatments understand this all too well.

Since the '60's, anxiety has been regarded by the medical and psychiatric communities as a biochemical disorder, best treated with medications. Psychologists and psychotherapists have labeled anxiety as a malfunction in an individual's thinking or "*belief system.*" Some still believe anxiety to be the result of repressed memories or emotions. Phobias have been regarded as marginal disorders, related usually to irrational fears of animals or insects.

Until recently, no one imagined how drastically anxiety was restricting millions of people's lives, preventing them from engaging in normal activities such as driving, eating in public or shopping. Very few suspected that millions of professional careers were being devastated or severely restricted by the inability to fly, to drive or to give public speeches.

The medical and psychological communities did not realize that helping people overcome anxiety disorders, anxiety attacks and phobias would be a principal goal for therapists in the '90's. The health care community came face-to-face with this monumental challenge, unprepared.

It is well documented that anxiety disorders, such as anxiety attacks, are frequently misdiagnosed. It is misdiagnosed as *agitated depression, bipolar disorder, angina, inner ear disease, allergic reactions, hyper or hypothyroidism . . .* the list is endless. The National Institute of Mental Health states that a person who suffers from anxiety attacks sees, on the average, 10 health care professionals before being accurately diagnosed.

The problem is that many physicians are reluctant to refer these patients to mental health professionals. They see these patients with their many physical complaints as having an *"organically based"* problem.

In fairness to some physicians, high levels of anxiety cause an array of physical symptoms that can mimic physical illnesses. These patients usually see physicians on the average of 37.3 times a year, as opposed to 5 times a year for the general population. People with anxiety disorders are highly suggestible and therefore can be all-too-willing subjects for extensive and costly medical testing and treatment. Usually, after elaborate testing (and thousands of dollars later), they receive a *"clean bill of health"*.

Anxiety is rarely addressed as the real cause for their

many physical symptoms. Their patients repeated visits and phone calls to be *"reassured"* that their persistent physical symptoms are not a sign of an impending heart attack or cancer are minimized as hypochondria and their physical complaints are not viewed as symptoms of high levels of anxiety.

Finally, those physicians who do diagnosis an anxiety disorder in their patients often send them to mental health professionals whose understanding of anxiety is inadequate. The health care community has, for too long, tried to transfer the clinical and physical precepts for the treatment of depression into something workable for treating anxiety.

For years the psychiatric community has been pushing *"square pegs into round holes"* when it comes to treating anxiety disorders. Our clients are telling us daily, that it doesn't fit. **The significant connection that most psychotherapists miss in treating clients with anxiety disorders, is the relationship between avoidance and general anxiety.**

First, they overlook or minimize the amount of avoidance the anxiety sufferer is using to control their anxiety. This leads them to mistakenly associate the medication or therapy with the reduction of anxiety attacks. Whereas, it is the patient's *avoidance* behavior that is controlling these anxiety episodes.

Second, in overlooking the relationship between avoidance and anxiety, many professionals are unknowingly crippling their clients by encouraging them to avoid stressful activities until they *"feel better"* or *"get to the root of their problem"* in insight therapy, or until they have mastered *"changing their thinking"* to a more positive or rational level.

Anxiety attack sufferers are often encouraged to leave stressful jobs, not to drive on freeways or to avoid people who are difficult to deal with. This type of advice increases (by endorsement) the avoidance that escalates general anxiety levels. The focus becomes "*how to do less*" instead of "*how to do more.*" And when an anxious person avoids, the smaller and more unsafe their world appears.

This book is about helping anxious people. It's about reevaluating methods and models used in the treatment of anxiety disorders. Treating anxiety in the same way we treat depression only gives marginal results. It is time to take a closer look at the most frequent client any medical doctor, psychiatrist, or counselor has in their practice today, the client who suffers from *anxiety*!

Cynthia Scott, M.S.

Chapter 1

LEARNING ABOUT ANXIETY ATTACKS

Mary: Anxiety attacks in the kitchen

In 1979, while working as a counselor at a mental health center in Mississippi, I met my first client with anxiety attacks. Mary, a twenty-eight year old woman, walked into our center one afternoon crying uncontrollably. The only coherent statement she could give me for several minutes was that she was "going crazy" and she had to get out of her house. I let her cry, and after about ten minutes, she was able to talk to me.

She self-consciously told me she was the mother of three children and that she stayed at home while her husband worked at a nearby plant. Several months ago she began to have sudden overwhelming feelings that something dreadful was about to happen. When these feelings occurred, her hands would tremble and her heart would beat wildly. When she had these feelings, no matter where she might be, she would have to "get out and get out quickly." This happened in various unrelated situations. It happened in grocery stores, restaurants, sometimes driving and lately it began to occur in her kitchen. Because of this, she was now unable to drive, grocery shop or prepare meals for her family.

Her condition was very upsetting because she had always enjoyed cooking and trying new recipes she found in magazines. She was now avoiding going into the kitchen as much as possible.

Lately, she would go into the kitchen in the morning and gather enough food to feed her children during the day. She would then take the food and leave it on the living room coffee table, so as to avoid added trips to the kitchen.

Her husband was cooking supper every evening and even

with his help, she could barely manage to stay in the kitchen long enough to wash dishes afterwards. Her condition had been getting progressively worse, and that morning she started to have the same feelings in her living room. This new development is what brought her to the center.

I did not know at the time that Mary had an anxiety disorder, and was having anxiety attacks. But I knew that to help her, it would be essential to restore, as quickly as possible, Mary's normal abilities to drive, shop and cook. I instinctively knew that in Mary's case she didn't need "talk" therapy she needed "action".

When someone loses faith in their ability to do the everyday activities of life such as driving, shopping, cooking or participating in activities with family or friends, a serious consequence happens almost immediately. Their self-confidence as a normal person who can competently handle the routine tasks of life, diminishes. To reestablish this competency, as quickly as possible, is essential for their well being. To accomplish this, it is important that they understand how the disability occurred, how to correct it, and how to prevent it from happening again.

Self-confidence is built on our knowledge that we can handle whatever problems life hands us. All people quickly become immobilized when faced with problems they can't solve. Confidence is restored when their understanding and their competency are regained!

Anxiety is Not an Emotion You Can "Think" Your Way Out Of

I quickly learned that the traditional methods of treatment I had learned in college did not work with Mary. Having to "fly by the seat of my pants" I discovered she was unable to "think her way out of her problem." Her insights and thoughts were useless in lowering her anxiety since her normal thinking was seriously "disabled" by her high level of anxiety. But I learned she could "**do**" **her way out of anxiety, and then the correct reasoning quickly followed.** This was a major discovery for me and for Mary.

I learned that avoidance was the common denominator in her failure to help herself. I also learned that by taking *small successful steps* toward what she was avoiding, her confidence improved. And, of much greater importance to me, **with each successful step her general anxiety level was reduced and with it her anxious thinking.** I saw Mary for three months and, with an action-oriented treatment plan, she was able to recover.

Over the next fifteen years I would treat hundreds more with anxiety attacks, all having developed strong patterns of avoidance, resulting in diminished life styles, increased general anxiety and thus lower self-confidence. Each of them had tried one or more of the following treatments: medication, "insight" therapy, expressive therapy, group therapy, cognitive therapy, hypnosis, bio-feedback and/or relaxation treatment with little or marginal results.

My husband Stan (also a psychotherapist) and I have been specializing in and successfully treating people who have anxiety disorders for over ten years. We have found that anxiety attacks are very treatable and can be eliminated in a brief period of time - between three weeks and three months. We have designed a treatment model called *"field work"* that eliminates the need for medication maintenance, the struggle to change one's thinking to be more "positive" or "rational," or investigating one's childhood memories to make them feel less anxious. We hope by making this book brief and in plain language that you can understand anxiety, how it works, and what it is telling you.

The common theme you will need to remember is - *anxiety is not an emotion you can "think" your way out of.* Hopefully, this book will provide those of you who suffer from anxiety attacks the action-based approach you need to recover.

The following chapters of this book will describe why anxiety attacks occur and who is likely to develop them (Chapter

2), how anxiety effects you physically and mentally (Chapter 3), how avoidance increases your general anxiety level (Chapter 4 & 5).

We would also like to assert that this book is a self-help book and is not intended as a replacement for professional therapy. Many who read this book will need professional help, so we have included information on what treatment for anxiety attacks should look like (Chapter 6 & 7), a section on how intimidation is related to anxiety attacks (Chapter 8), a section on how anxiety effects thinking (Chapter 9), and the problems of other treatment methods in treating anxiety attacks (Chapter 10).

These chapters can guide you in choosing appropriate professional help if you find you need it.

Chapter 2

DE-MYSTIFYING ANXIETY ATTACKS

Jill's First Anxiety Attack

Jill had been an office manager in a doctor's office for three years. It was a fast-paced, good-paying job. She enjoyed going to work each day. One day, as she was assisting the doctor in a routine procedure, her palms got sweaty and she began to feel dizzy. She kept working, hoping these feelings would pass, but it seemed the longer she worked the dizzier she felt.

She left the room for a break and noticed her heartbeat was accelerated, and she had a hot smothering kind of feeling. The walls seemed to close in around her oddly, and she felt if she didn't get out of the building for some fresh air she would "lose it." Getting out of the building was a necessity. As she rushed outside she began to feel more calm.

After a few minutes, she felt more in control and was able to return to work. Confused and emotionally drained, she completed her day's work but was worried about what had happened to her. The next day at work she began to wonder "Will it happen again, and if it does will it be worse?" She felt uncomfortable just going into the room where she had the strange feelings. By the end of the week she was having someone else to do all the assisting when the doctor worked in that particular room. Every time she went into that room she felt uncomfortable. Jill wasn't sure why she associated the room with what happened to her. All she was certain of is that she did not want to have that awful experience again.

* * *

Jill has just had her first anxiety attack. She is understandably alarmed and bewildered. **Jill has just had a report card from her body on how well she is doing emotionally.** She doesn't understand it quite in this way yet, but hopefully she will soon. Jill is one of the three million people in the U.S. who will have a similar experience this year.

Unfortunately, she will have several more similar experiences before she will accidentally find a magazine with an article on anxiety attacks. Or, unexpectedly talk to another person who has had the same experience. Or, she will find a health care professional who knows about anxiety disorders. She will discover that the symptoms are almost the same for everyone . . . dizziness, shortness of breath, feelings of being smothered, choking, trembling hands, heart palpitations, ringing in the ears, nausea or diarrhea, sweaty palms or numbness in the extremities and sometimes chest pains.

We're going to come back to Jill, but for now let's talk about why Jill and millions of others, had their first anxiety attack. Then we'll explain in Chapter 4 why, after all their efforts, they continue to have them. But, you can't understand the second or the third anxiety attack without first understanding where the "first" one came from. It has a story all its own.

"Why do I have anxiety attacks? These panicky feelings that just seem to come out of nowhere?" We hear this question in our practice every day. By the time our clients reach us, they have already gotten the typical (and misleading) answers such as:

. . . "You have a chemical imbalance that should be treated with medication."

. . . "It's just stress and you need to learn how to relax. Take a vacation, everything will pass."

. . . "You were probably molested as a child, or experienced some other trauma. Once you remember and deal with the trauma, your anxiety attacks will go away. Or, "Your anxiety attacks are repressed anger towards your parents or spouse."

. . . "Your thinking shows an irrational belief system. Once you change your thinking patterns, your anxiety level will come down."

. . . "You have a (*fill in the blank*) disease which I happen to have a specialty in treating."

It is possible that some of these issues may apply to you. Because of your anxiety, your brain chemistry may be out of balance. You might have had a significant trauma as a child. You probably need to learn to relax. You may be angry with your spouse or your parents. But these are not the reasons you have anxiety attacks.

How Do Anxiety Attacks Begin?

Our experience of successfully treating clients with anxiety attacks brings us to a much simpler answer. We use a simple, but informative, demonstration to teach people how their anxiety attacks first began and what they are doing to perpetuate them. It will be helpful and enlightening for you to try this demonstration yourself. This one small demonstration will teach you an encyclopedia of information about anxiety attacks. So take the time to do it for yourself.

You will need a large pitcher of water, a glass, and a bowl to set the glass in. First fill your glass 1/3 full.

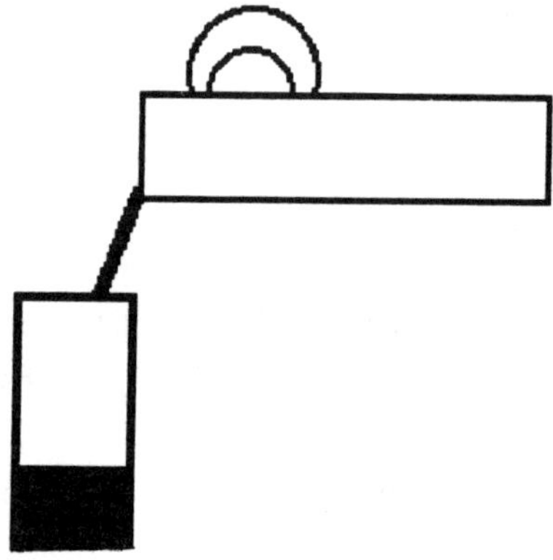

This 1/3 full level of water represents a "normal" level of anxiety. This low level of water represents the level of anxiety we need to remember the common "have to's" of everyday life. Things like remembering to pay our bills on time, remembering dates or important appointments, remembering to lock our doors at night or stop at red lights, etc. This is the "normal" level of anxiety we all need, to function safely and effectively in everyday routine situations.

Now, people who have anxiety attacks fill your glass with water a little higher than half way full.

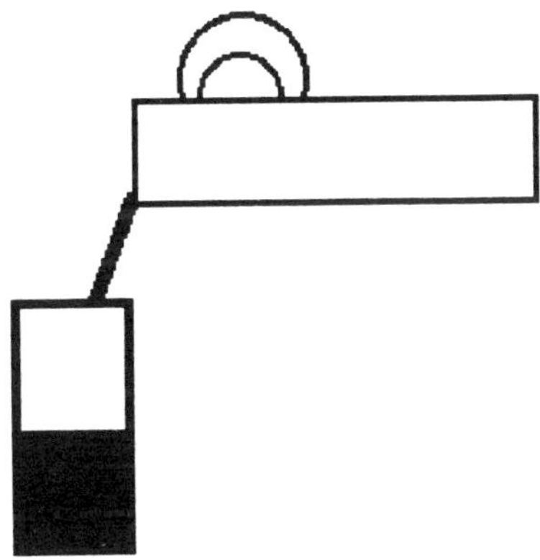

This slightly higher water level represents the general anxiety level of people who have anxiety attacks. This is a constant, "wake-up-with-it" everyday level. People who develop anxiety attacks function at this level of anxiety regardless of whether they are in a stressful situation or not.

Sound familiar? Some people call it "hyper" or high strung.

A lot of interesting things happen when someone has an anxiety level this high. People who function at this level are highly motivated people. If they work, they have a reputation for being dependable, responsible, a "can-do" sort of person. They're well thought of, and are usually successful in their careers. They like to "be prepared." And this level of anxiety provides them with the extra energy to take care of things or advance in their careers.

They are "the buck stops here" sort of person. Everyone wants them on their team because they'll get the job done. They are usually caretakers of others' emotions. People come to them with their problems. They will usually "go the extra mile" in friendships, with their coworkers, or in family relations. So there are a lot of associated benefits that go along with an anxiety level this high.

However, during one's mid-20's or early 30's these individuals begin to develop the physical side effects of operating at higher levels of anxiety for extended lengths of time. They start to experience headaches, migraines, heartburn, low back pain, ulcers, high blood pressure, and constant fatigue. These are all messages from your body telling you, that you are living with a high level of anxiety . . . and with very little relief.

Your body tries to be as clear as it can with you. Your aches and pains are the first *"notes from your teacher"*. And you know what that usually means . . . If you don't take care of things, there will be stronger messages later on.

So you say "O.K., I'm going to practice stress management, maybe exercise more, stop smoking, drink less coffee, or lose some weight and try to get my stress down." But what usually happens is . . . life throws some unexpected (but not unusual) little surprises your way. Get your water pitcher ready. For every upsetting experience you had before your first anxiety attack, drop a big splash of water into your glass...

A divorce, separation or problems in an important relationship (coworkers or children)...

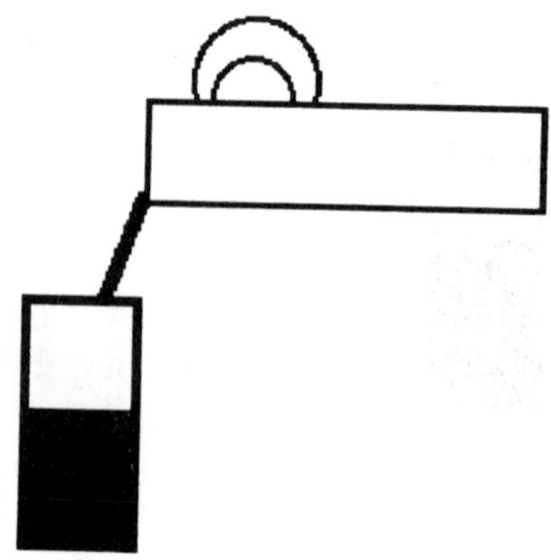

Unexpected car repairs. ("I thought you said you put the oil cap back on?!")

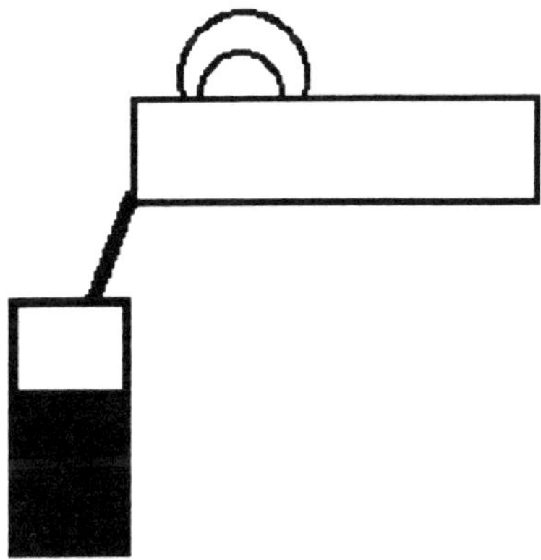

April 15th . . . ("Do you mean we can't take that deduction?!")

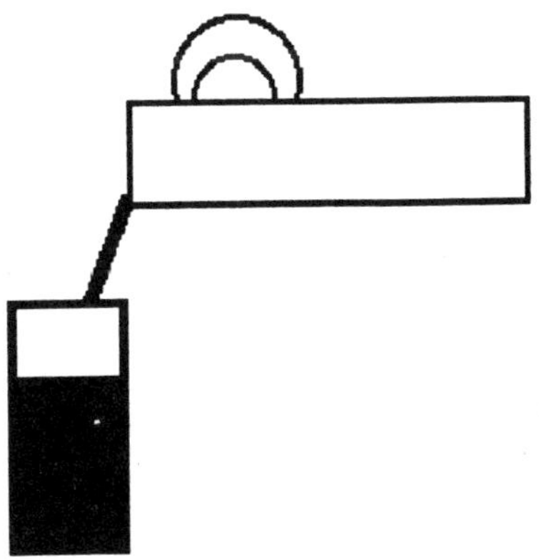

A birth in your immediate family. ("We need a bigger house!")

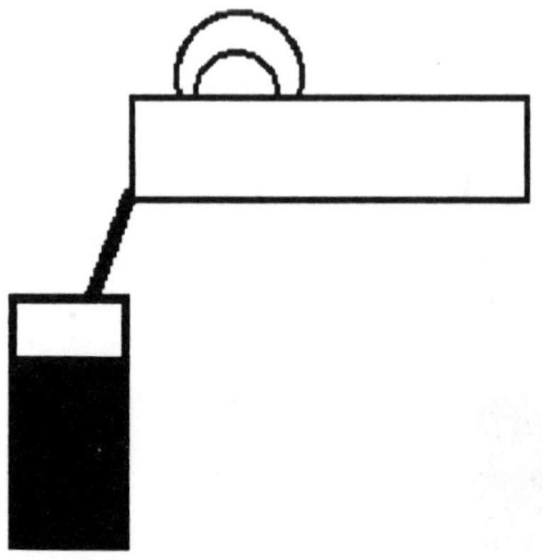

A new job or transfer to a new office. ("But this is the second transfer in three years!")

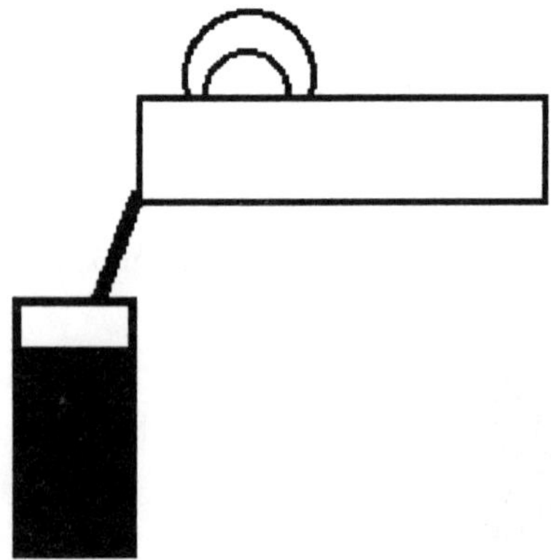

A continuing problem with the boss or co-worker. ("You need the report by when?")

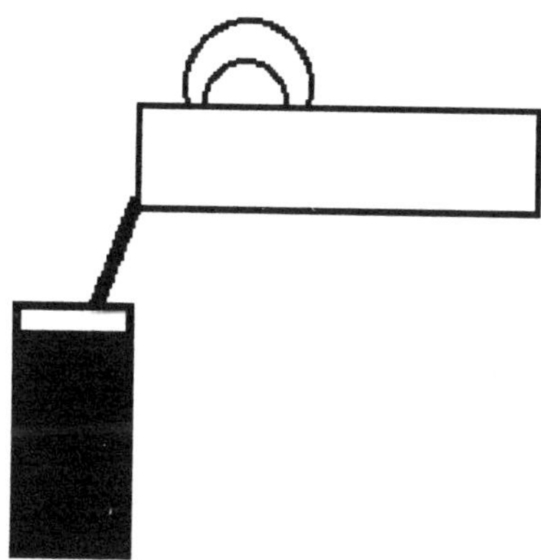

New job responsibilities requiring more skills and involving more stress. ("But I hate computers!")

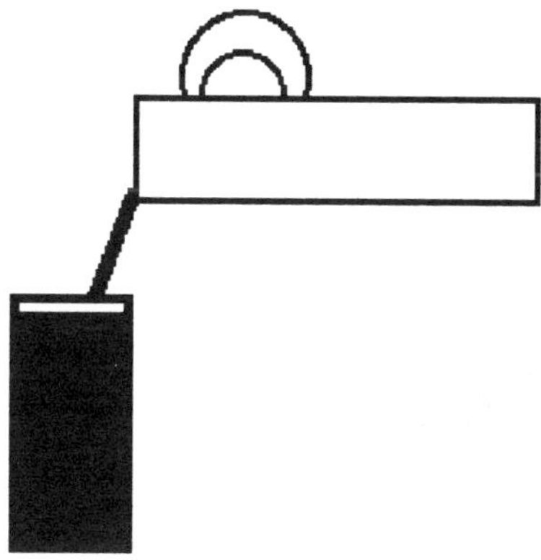

An illness or death in the family...

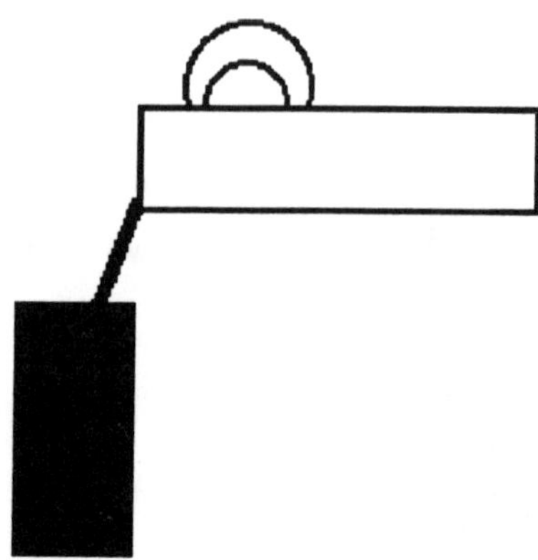

Visiting relatives! A flat tire! A confrontation with your spouse! The Boss Wants To See You! Your report wasn't accepted! Company coming for dinner! How much was the electric bill? A crowded freeway!

***

And your glass OVERFLOWS. Your heart races, your hands tremble and palms sweat, you feel disoriented, dizzy, and have overwhelming thoughts of dying or going crazy.

The overflow is the anxiety attack. It's not dangerous, you won't die, but it is an experience that raises your general anxiety level and frightens you. An anxiety attack is giving you two very clear messages from your body.

Message No. 1: Your general anxiety level is extremely high, and has been for some time.

Take Jill for example . . . Jill was an excellent employee. She was very responsible and reliable at work. She made sure the office ran smoothly. Even on her days off, she stocked other co-workers' stations and often did their jobs. She could do it faster than she could train them. If someone needed to be off for an afternoon, it was Jill they would call because Jill would make sure things were taken care of. At annual parties Jill took the responsibility for making sure there were refreshments, often staying up late the night before to make the office "favorite." She took care of her house and family in the same manner. If she added an activity, she never subtracted one.

Jill was well thought of and was paid well and she would be the first to say she earned every penny. She "earned" a very high level of anxiety as well. She woke up *"with this level,"* ate lunch *"with this level"* and went to bed *"with this level."* She was working her way into her first anxiety attack.

Message No. 2: You have just gone through a series of unexpected, unplanned situations that drew on emotional reserves you did not have.

Jill's life for the past several years had been emotionally trying. She recently had her second child, she had been promoted to office manager, and her husband was worried about losing his job due to down-sizing in his company. Her family was pressuring her to have their elderly aunt move in with her and her husband because, "they had the biggest house." Due to a fender-bender, her insurance company had thrown her into a high risk group with larger insurance payments. Christmas bills were beginning to come in and they were more than expected.

Jill's first anxiety attack was a painful, poignant message to her. The water demonstration makes Jill's first anxiety attack predictable and comprehensible. If Jill's general anxiety level had been lower when she experienced those ordinary (but stress producing) "extra" events she had not planned on, her anxiety level would not have risen to the point of overflow. But, by depleting her emotional reserves, Jill was a prime candidate for an anxiety attack when the next "unexpected" event came her way.

A Profile of People Who Develop Anxiety Attacks

We are often asked, "Are there people who are predisposed to develop anxiety attacks?" We believe so. People who develop anxiety attacks show clear and consistent traits in handling their life and relationships in a particular manner. These traits contribute to the beginning or basic "higher than normal" anxiety level we spoke of in the water glass demonstration.

People who develop anxiety attacks:

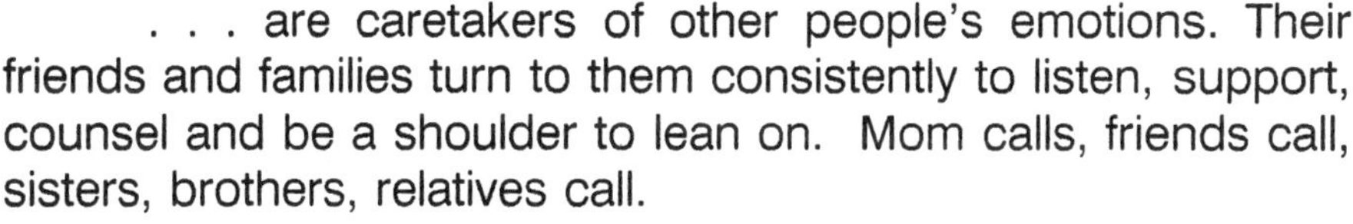

. . . are caretakers of other people's emotions. Their friends and families turn to them consistently to listen, support, counsel and be a shoulder to lean on. Mom calls, friends call, sisters, brothers, relatives call.

. . . are caretakers of other people's problems. Often viewed as dependable, responsible, "the buck stops here" kind of person. The last person out of the office. "Call so-so she'll get it done," kind of group member. "I've got too much work to do; I can't call in sick," employee.

. . . are perfectionists. Ninety-nine percent right is not good enough. They focus on the 1% that can be done better.

. . . are overly accommodating in personal relationships. "He didn't really mean to be rude to me, he's just going through a rough time and I need to be more understanding." "She's always late, but that's just her personality, so I don't need to get angry about it."

. . . go 110 miles an hour all day, every day. "Yes, I think I can fit that in, after I get home from work, take the boys to baseball practice, fix dinner, wash clothes and do a report for work."

Yes, there are traits that lead to that "higher than normal" anxiety level that sets the stage for having an anxiety attack. Can you say "That's me!" to three of these traits? If so, your general everyday anxiety level is probably higher than it should be. If you're already having anxiety attacks, this is one of the reasons why. Remember, the foundation for anxiety attacks lies in these traits, and with the right outside stressful "surprises," you have just the necessary combination for trouble.

So when clients ask us, "Where do anxiety attacks come from?", we have ready information for them. Your anxiety attack is a very clear message. It says, "you're emotionally overdrawn!" You've taken on too much in too little time. You've tried to accommodate too many people without regard for your own emotional supplies.

The first anxiety attack does not come out of the blue. The first anxiety attack is as predictable as getting an overdraft notice from your bank when you write checks beyond what you've deposited. An anxiety attack is much the same information sent by your body . . . **You are emotionally overdrawn!**

Chapter 3

UNDERSTANDING YOUR ANXIETY IN MEASURABLE TERMS

Marcie started having anxiety attacks when she was 29 years old. She had read in a woman's magazine that they were "controllable" with medication. So she made an appointment with her doctor. Her physician told her that very little was known about why anxiety attacks occurred. It was thought that they were probably the result of a chemical imbalance.

He suggested she try some medication to see if he could find one that would stop the anxiety attacks. She tried several different kinds, some in combination. Nothing seemed to take away the awful "not knowing" of when or where she might have another anxiety attack.

The watching and waiting for the next one was the worst part. Marcie was constantly apprehensive. "If I just had some warning it wouldn't be so bad." She felt she could handle her situation better if she could just "predict" when she might have another attack.

* * *

Of all the frightening things in the world, hurricanes, tornados, earthquakes, even death, none are as frightening as the ones we can't predict. Being able to predict and understand the things that happen to us is one of the ways we feel more in control of our lives. We've all heard people say, *"If I just had more information, I'd feel better."* We believe this type of information is also necessary for those who have anxiety attacks.

In spite of the health care community's general lack of knowledge about the cause of anxiety attacks, we have not found them to be mysterious, unexplainable, or unpredictable. Anxiety attacks are an understandable, measurable and predictable report card from your body on your emotional health. Particularly, it is a report on how anxious your life is becoming on a daily basis.

In order for you to understand what your anxiety is telling you, you will need a *"tool"* such as a good old fashioned measuring stick to decipher its code for you. Here is a simple example of a useful tool.

* * *

My mother is an interior designer. I always marveled how she could "visualize" the way furniture would fit into a room. I would come home from school and our furniture would always be in different places. I had no idea how she knew what would go where. She always seemed to know before she moved a chair or a table whether it would fit or not.

After I moved into my first apartment, she came to visit me one weekend. I was in the middle of decorating and she had come to help. She watched with some dismay as I began to move furniture around the room trying to figure out where different pieces would go. I explained, as I worked, how I just didn't seem to have the *"understanding"* of spatial relations the way she did. I had to physically *move* the furniture to tell where it would fit.

My mother smiled as she told me to stop moving that heavy furniture and get her a tape measure. With the tape measure in hand, she quickly measured off the furniture. She then asked for sheets of newspaper. She took the newspaper and folded it in squares the approximate size of each piece of furniture. Then, she looked up and said *"Now where do you want to try your couch?"*

I laughingly answered, *"Let's try over there first."* We moved the newspaper squares around the room as we tried every piece of furniture on every wall.

* * *

Simple enough? Certainly easier moving *"paper"* furniture than the heavy counterpart, right? My mother had given me a *"tool"*.

As I got older (and moved more furniture) I began to get better at predicting where my furniture would look best. But until I had the *"tool,"* that profound secret my mother shared with me, I'd still be pushing and tugging on heavy furniture to make it fit. Yes, with my *"tool,"* the incomprehensible world of spatial relations became much clearer.

You, will need a tool also to help you understand your anxiety so you can predict or know in advance when you are vulnerable to an anxiety attack.

A Simple Tool . . . The Anxiety Scale

The first step we take in therapy with a new client is to explain our anxiety scale and how to use it. This gives us some *"common ground"* to discuss their anxiety level, or how anxious they are feeling. It's very simple:

1 2 3 4 5 6 7 8 9 10
CALM I----------------------------------I PANIC

Our scale goes from one to ten, with one being how you feel when you are very calm, and ten being how you feel when you have an anxiety attack. Many things happen to you as your anxiety moves across the scale. It's important for you to understand that you not only *"feel"* differently as your anxiety increases or decreases but you also *"think"* differently.

At a Level 1, you physically feel comfortable, relaxed, rested, with all your muscles loose. You also *"think"* a certain way. You recognize no problems that you can't handle. You have thoughts of well-being or satisfaction with yourself, maybe peaceful thoughts about your life.

The way you feel and the way you think changes as your anxiety goes up and down. Each anxiety level brings a different kind of physical feeling and a different kind of thinking. We will go through each level and describe what changes these levels usually bring.

When we describe the physical symptoms of each anxiety level, your own symptoms may be different. Not everyone will feel sweaty palms at a Level 6. Some may never have sweaty palms. But we feel you'll be able to substitute your own symptoms when they differ from the ones we list.

We would like you to pay close attention to how your thoughts and physical experience change as your anxiety goes higher. The emotional thinking at each level will be more accurate. People usually think similarly at each level of anxiety although their physical bodies will "*talk*" to them in different ways. Just a word of encouragement; you may find reading the list of symptoms anxiety-provoking. This is a normal response. It is part of our "*human sensitivity*" to respond emotionally to things we have had some experience with ourselves.

Ask any woman who has had a baby to read a passage on what happens during childbirth. She will respond both emotionally and physically to what she reads. If you have had anxiety attacks, expect to respond with some degree of change in your own physical symptoms as well as in the way you think.

It is best to read what you can, then, simply **stop** if you're uncomfortable. Then, come back and read the rest when you're comfortable again. Let's review our anxiety scale to understand the physical symptoms and emotional thinking that happens at each level of anxiety. Please feel free to change the physical symptoms to fit your own experience with anxiety.

LEVEL 1

1 2 3 4 5 6 7 8 9 10
X---------------------------------------I

PHYSICAL: Your muscles are relaxed at this level, and your "*body*" is usually forgotten about.

THOUGHTS: At this level your thoughts are peaceful, and you have no recognition of problems. *"Everything is going smoothly just like I knew it would."*

LEVEL 2

1 2 3 4 5 6 7 8 9 10
I---X------------------------------------I

PHYSICAL: Still, you have no conscious body awareness. If there is any awareness, it is one of comfort or relaxation.

THOUGHTS: At this level your thoughts are still peaceful. Thoughts usually move easily from one subject of interest to another. *"I wonder where we'll vacation this year?"*

LEVEL 3

1 2 3 4 5 6 7 8 9 10
I--------X--------------------------------I

PHYSICAL: Because the anxiety is a little higher there is more awareness of the body at this level. However, there is no discomfort, just recognition of movement and muscle tone.

THOUGHTS: Your thoughts at this level of anxiety include becoming slightly more aware of your surrounding environment.

Whereas, at earlier levels you seem to daydream, thoughts at this level are focused on what you are doing at the time. Maybe doing a favorite hobby, or some task you can do well, or are familiar with. *"I have always enjoyed doing this, it's so relaxing."*

LEVEL 4

1 2 3 4 5 6 7 8 9 10
I-----------X---------------------------I

PHYSICAL: At this anxiety level you feel *"energized."* Muscles are beginning to tighten, ready for action. Adrenalin begins to pump and you feel the physical signs of anticipation. But, because this is not an overwhelming feeling, you can still concentrate.

THOUGHTS: Thoughts at this anxiety level focus on what is going on around you. Slight interest or anticipation begins here. This is a pleasant feeling of being in control. If there is *"something"* about to happen in your environment you feel a positive competence about the encounter. You can still rationalize the *"unknown"* as something you can handle. *"I can't wait until we start. I know I can do this!"*

LEVEL 5

1 2 3 4 5 6 7 8 9 10
I----------------X----------------------I

PHYSICAL: At this level, breathing becomes a little irregular. You begin to feel the effects of adrenalin. This point begins the first negative labeling, *"I'm feeling nervous."* All body functions speed up a small amount, and you begin to get sensitized to things going on around you.

THOUGHTS: Thoughts at this level, begin to focus on the amount of physical symptoms happening in your body. The ability to concentrate has not been effected yet, but your attention span is short. Feelings of impatience begin. You begin to have sporadic thoughts of insecurity, but are still able to rationalize that you can handle whatever it is. *"This is really going to take some concentration, but if I'm careful I'll pull it off."*

LEVEL 6

1 2 3 4 5 6 7 8 9 10
I--------------------X-------------------I

PHYSICAL: At this level, adrenalin is pumping heavily and the physical symptoms become stronger and more acute. Palms sweat, muscles become tighter, sporadic dizziness or light-headedness, sometimes trembling in the hands occurs. The body demands more attention and the energy (adrenalin) in the body needs an *"outlet."*

THOUGHTS: Thoughts at this level focus on trying to cope with the growing feelings of "*dangerousness*" in your surroundings. You try to ignore the physical symptoms you are noticing in your body. This makes concentration difficult, your body is demanding attention, and so is your environment. Negative thought start to become catastrophic. *"I'm scared I'm not going to be able to handle this! What if I lose control?"* The "*what if*" thinking means the ability to rationalize is impaired. The emotion of "*impatience*" begins here. "*Why can't we start?*"

LEVEL 7

1 2 3 4 5 6 7 8 9 10
I-------------------------X--------------I

PHYSICAL: All physical symptoms become more acute. Lights become brighter, sounds become louder, and muscle tension intensifies (sometimes causing nervous spasm).

THOUGHTS: Physical symptoms cannot be ignored, and catastrophic thinking *"runs the show."* Thoughts of impending disaster run through all thinking. *"If I don't get out of here, I'm going to lose control!"* At this level, all self-confidence is gone. The ability to rationalize that *"nothing will probably happen"* is gone.

LEVEL 8

1 2 3 4 5 6 7 8 9 10
I------------------------------X----------I

PHYSICAL: At this level the amount of adrenalin being pumped into the body causes many more physical symptoms. Nausea, heart palpitations and stomach aches are some of the more upsetting physical symptoms.

THOUGHTS: More catastrophic thinking, the ability to see any way out is gone. Survival becomes the goal. *"I'll never make it out of here! If I do I'll never do this again!"* Patience is gone, rescue must be soon, or a disaster is foreseen.

LEVEL 9

1 2 3 4 5 6 7 8 9 10
I-----------------------------------X-----I

PHYSICAL: Many of the symptoms that mimic other physical illnesses or problems occur at this level. They are usually so extreme that they "*alarm*" you into going to the emergency room. Anxiety attack sufferers are frequent visitors to E.R. hospitals. Some of the more frightening symptoms are numbness in the extremities, chest pains, and hyperventilation.

THOUGHTS: *"I'm out of control! I knew this would happen!" "Someone help me! I'm going to pass out!"*

LEVEL 10

1 2 3 4 5 6 7 8 9 10
I---X

PHYSICAL: *OVERLOAD!*

THOUGHTS: *PANIC! "I'm going to die!"*

Many of you may have found that even reading through the anxiety scale is uncomfortable. As your anxiety escalates, neither the "*thinking*" nor the physical symptoms are pleasant. However, the process must be scrutinized for you to have an understanding of how anxiety affects your physical symptoms, *and thinking.* By understanding the different levels of anxiety you can begin to understand your thoughts and feelings.

Most anxiety sufferers just feel anxious. But, by using the anxiety scale as a tool to define your anxiety, you can break anxiety into parts you can understand. Then your thoughts and feelings are not so mysterious and unpredictable. The more you are able to label your anxious feelings into something more definable such as a Level 6 or a Level 7, the easier it becomes to recognize when your anxiety is escalating, and to see **catastrophic thinking as a "*symptom*" instead of the "*cause*" of your anxiety.**

Taking Your Anxiety Temperature

A good way to practice the anxiety scale is to practice what we call *"taking your anxiety temperature"* during the day, which means to take time during the day to stop and notice, where on the scale your anxiety is, at that moment.

If it is higher than a Level 5.5, stop what you are doing and take a five to ten minute break to let your anxiety come down. During this break is a good time to practice deep breathing or relaxation, if these are techniques that you feel comfortable doing.

A good technique for practicing using the anxiety scale is to place a piece of non-transparent tape on your watch. Since most people have a habit of looking at their watch several times a day, every time you look at your watch and see the tape, check your anxiety level. Do this simple technique for one day to become familiar with using the scale. Again, the anxiety scale is a smart way to start understanding your anxiety in measurable terms. Most people don't realize how high their level is all the time, but by taking your anxiety *"temperature"* you can become more aware of your everyday level.

Chapter 4

AVOIDANCE: THE CRIPPLING QUICK FIX

Ninety percent of the clients that come to us for anxiety attacks have been on medication or involved in some kind of psychotherapy or both. Most have spent much money and put an enormous amount of trust in the Health Care community hoping to *"get well."*

They are still very anxious. Almost all are still having anxiety attacks or, if not, they are having to *restrict* their lives to an incredible degree in order *not* to have them. So, what's wrong? They're going to educated professionals who, on the average, have good answers for most questions.

Traditional theory (most commonly taught to professionals) proposes that anxiety comes from strongly repressed emotion or that it is the result of a chemical imbalance. Depending on who you see, someone trained in psychology or someone trained in medicine, you will either receive therapy to "*unleash*" your repressed emotions or medication to "*correct*" your chemical imbalance.

The unfortunate result of these therapies is a low rate of successful recovery. We will have more on why these treatment methods give only marginal results in Chapter 10, but for now, let's talk about a model that works.

Anxiety and avoidance. What is the relationship? Most of our clients tell us that if they didn't feel so anxious they wouldn't need to avoid.

Michelle, a recent client, put it like this. *"My anxiety takes away all my motivation to try again."* Michelle has been having anxiety attacks for over a year. Her first anxiety attack was in her car on the way to work. Soon, every time she got in her car she began to feel uncomfortable. And as driving became more difficult, she began to ask her husband to take her to work. She also noticed she was having *"anxious times"* at other places; at home and in large stores. Frightened by her escalating anxiety level she decided she needed to "*do*" less. It seemed the only rational conclusion.

Soon, her husband was having to do the grocery shopping because the bright lights and noise in the store made her anxious. Michelle decided to go to her doctor. He told her that her hormones were out of balance and gave her medication to "*correct*" them.

When this didn't help, she went to a psychologist who told her she was grieving over her parent's recent divorce. He explained how she needed to recognize and express her feelings of anger and sadness about the divorce.

None of this seemed to make things any better. A month later Michelle quit trying to approach her problem. Overwhelmed by her failed attempts to help herself, she finally quit her job. Michelle was completely housebound when she first heard of our center and called us.

Michelle didn't realize it, but when she began to avoid she was setting up a pattern which would further disable her. In Michelle's defense, many people were encouraging her to lower her anxiety level by not doing as much. She believed she had done everything she could to help herself. Michelle tried to continue her normal activities on her own. She also went to two different health-care professionals to get help for her anxiety attacks. We feel Michelle was not totally at fault for her worsening condition.

She was a bright, successful young woman. She was married, she had friends, and a supportive family that didn't mind going out of their way to make things easier for her. Her first question to us was: *"How did I get myself into this situation?"*

It was our first task to reassure her that it was not out of weakness or a physiological deficit that she was having anxiety attacks. Many normal daily stressors cause anxiety attacks.

After that, it is a matter of who gets quick *knowledgeable* intervention. That makes the difference between who becomes disabled and who rebounds quickly from their first anxiety attack.

WHAT THE HEALTH CARE COMMUNITY DOES NOT KNOW ABOUT ANXIETY. . . CAN HURT YOU

A study by Swinson, M.D., Soulios, M.D., Cox, M.A. & Kuch, M.D. (Am J Psychiatry 149:, July 1992) of anxiety attack patients treated at an emergency room, found that those patients who were instructed **not** to avoid the situation where the anxiety attack occurred, showed a significant reduction in their anxiety attacks.

The study included 33 emergency room patients who met the diagnosis of panic disorder with agoraphobia. Sixteen of the patients **only received reassurance** that what they had experienced was an anxiety attack and that they had no physical problem.

Seventeen other patients also received reassurance about their anxiety attack, but they were instructed that ***"The best way to reduce their fear was to confront the situation in which the anxiety attack had occurred as soon as possible."*** The study found those patients who were reassured and instructed to confront their fear greatly improved. This group went from 2.53 down to 0.76 anxiety attacks a week, after a six months follow-up. While those patients who only received reassurance and not told to confront their fear became significantly worst. They increased from 2.50 up to 3.38 anxiety attacks a week over the same period.

This study shows what we have also found; that if Michelle, when her anxiety attacks first occurred, had been able to go to her physician or other health care professional, and had gotten basic information on anxiety attacks and instructions "*not to avoid*", she might not have had another anxiety attack.

At this point, it was up to us to show how some of her own attempts (avoidance) to ease her anxiety were hurting her. There was no need for Michelle to have to come this far on her own without appropriate information and instructions on anxiety attacks.

ANXIETY AND AVOIDANCE

After we have explained our anxiety scale to our new client, the first question we ask is, *"What are you avoiding in order not to have an anxiety attack?"*

We will usually hear such things as:

1. "I avoid going to large stores, so I don't go to malls, grocery stores or department stores."
2. "I avoid driving on freeways."
3. "I avoid eating out in restaurants."
4. "I avoid going anywhere without my medication."
5. "I avoid taking elevators unless they are the glass type, or the fully enclosed elevator."
6. "I avoid driving downtown because there is too much traffic."
7. "I avoid meetings where someone might ask me to speak."
8. "I avoid parties because I don't like to make small talk."
9. "I avoid eating in front of people."
10. "I avoid going places that I don't know where the rest rooms are."
11. "I avoid setting work limits at my job because they might not like it."

And the list goes on . . .

Sometimes we hear. *"Oh, I'm not really avoiding anything."* However, when we ask *"How many of these things are you doing alone?"* We hear, *"Oh, I can do anything when my husband, wife, son, mother, or a friend is with me. But, I probably wouldn't do them alone."* Or, perhaps they don't *avoid* these activities, but they don't like to do them unless they have to. **This, is avoidance also. A little less obvious, but avoidance nevertheless.**

What role does avoidance play in raising or lowering your anxiety? How does avoidance bring on the second or third anxiety attacks? Why is avoidance a *"crippling quick-fix"* for your anxiety? Let's go back to Michelle.

Michelle had her first anxiety attack in her car. This caused her general anxiety level to become elevated, which caused her to "*anticipate*" another attack. She's not sure if being in the car had anything to do with it, but she is thinking about it. So, she watches and waits. Having an anxiety attack is a very uncomfortable feeling and she wants to make sure she doesn't have another one.

Remember how the overflowing water glass predicted how the first anxiety attack happened? Let's go back to *it* again. It can also help us to understand why these attacks continue to happen. After an individual has their first anxiety attack, their general anxiety level is elevated. Anxiety attacks are frightening, and thus painful. Like Michelle, one becomes excessively watchful, looking for signs that would suggest another attack is about to happen. The individual is very aware at this point that their anxiety level is much higher than normal. So, fill your glass a little higher than half way.

As the days go on, Michelle begins to see that she is most anxious in her car. She decides she will be extra careful when she's driving. Maybe it was because she was driving in heavy traffic that brought on those awful feelings. She remembers all too well the racing heartbeat, sweaty palms, and shortness of breath. So, she decided not to drive on the freeways to work because of the rush-hour traffic.

"Rationally, it was probably a good idea to not drive on crowded freeways," she thought. She felt so much safer not driving on freeways, that she decided it would be O.K. to stay off of freeways all the time. But, what Michelle didn't realize, was that this immediate "quick fix" of relief was like a "tar baby," which would make it harder and harder for her to break away from the *immediate emotional relief* that avoidance brings.

She also didn't realize that she was *"paying for it"* (the immediate emotional relief) by having her general anxiety level go up. Every time she *"quick-fixes"* it's like poring more water in a glass.

Michelle had been hooked by the "*quick fix*" of avoidance. It seemed so simple and so reasonable, and she "*felt*" better, at least for a while. She had found no other solution that helped as much. She also discovered that she felt better when she didn't drive on busy streets and just drove down neighborhood streets. It's easy to understand how powerful *"quick fixing"* is when you understand that this is the only *"tool"* Michelle had for keeping herself from having another attack.

When she quit driving to work on freeways, her general anxiety went higher. Her general anxiety level was so high now that she was now beginning to get uncomfortable even on side streets.

Now she was having to avoid major streets and having to take out-of-the-way detours to get to work. **And every time she avoided** driving the freeway or major street, her water glass was getting fuller and fuller.

Each time she would avoid, her general anxiety would rise higher and higher and . . .

higher, and she would get closer and closer to her second anxiety attack . . . until, it finally happened . . .!

This is why we call avoidance the crippling *"quick fix,"* because it will immediately lower your anticipatory anxiety, but your general anxiety will go up. It's the immediate, "*Whew! I solved it this time,*" but soon after you begin to worry, *"But, will it happen next time?"* This is your general anxiety going up. This is the role avoidance plays in anxiety and anxiety attacks. **The more you avoid, the closer you are to having your second, third, fourth, fifth, etc . . . anxiety attack.**

We feel avoidance is, often, the only recourse that many people have. Unfortunately, when a person with anxiety attacks goes for professional help, the professional often, unknowingly, supports the avoidance; *"Take this medication. When you feel less anxious, try to do those things again."* *Or "When we get to the root of your childhood trauma, then the depression and anxiety will go away and you'll then be able to resume your normal activities again,* **six months to a year from now!**"

Most people don't understand, the more you avoid an activity, the more anxiety will surround it. For example, you learned to roller skate when you were a child and then for many years you had no reason to skate. If someone invited you to go roller skating next Saturday morning how would you feel? Anxious? Apprehensive? You become apprehensive even if you have good memories of roller skating. Imagine the anxiety if you have only bad memories? It is important to remember the first rule of anxiety when dealing with anxiety attacks.

AVOIDANCE = ANXIETY
or
"If you don't keep your foot in the water, you forget how shallow the water is."
or
"Absence (from a feared activity) does not make the heart grow fonder."

Why do we feel anxiety when we avoid? Why are we not satisfied with the thought, *"Oh, well that's just something I can't do, and that's O.K.?"* Self-confidence is built on feelings of competency, and on feelings of safety. It's easy to say, *"I can't play Mozart on the piano, or rebuild the engine of my car. That is just something I can't do, and that's O.K. too."* Our feelings of self-confidence are not challenged because our feelings of safety are not threatened. Most likely, no one will come up to us on Monday morning and say, *"Before you can get your pay check, or before you can buy groceries for your family, or before you take your son to football practice, you must learn how to play Mozart." Right?* The unlikeliness of it ensures our feelings of safety . . . and our feelings of self-confidence.

However, if we fear things that are common parts of everyday life such as eating with other people, driving alone, or shopping for groceries, then our feelings of safety will be challenged constantly. We can (and usually do) get asked to do these things on any normal day and have our feelings of safety threatened. This is why our general anxiety level escalates when we know we are not able to do something. We're constantly anticipating the next time we might have to perform, and then when we avoid it, our general anxiety level goes higher.

Unfortunately, the advice most people receive from family, friends and many helping professionals, is that if things are too stressful, stop fighting it.

"Just don't do it, if it makes you that anxious."

"The freeways are too dangerous anyway."

"You don't need to go to the grocery store; your husband can shop for you. Why should only women be responsible for grocery shopping?"

"You don't need to go to the shopping center and spend money right now anyway. It is better to save for the future."

"You don't need to keep that job. If your boss is overworking you; quit and find another job later."

This is, for the most part, well intentioned guidance. However, what it lacks is the understanding that all avoidance only raises one's anxiety . . . and lowers' one's feelings of self-confidence. As avoidance and anxiety are inextricably linked, so are anxiety and self-confidence (feelings of safety).

Avoidance and anxiety work together . . .

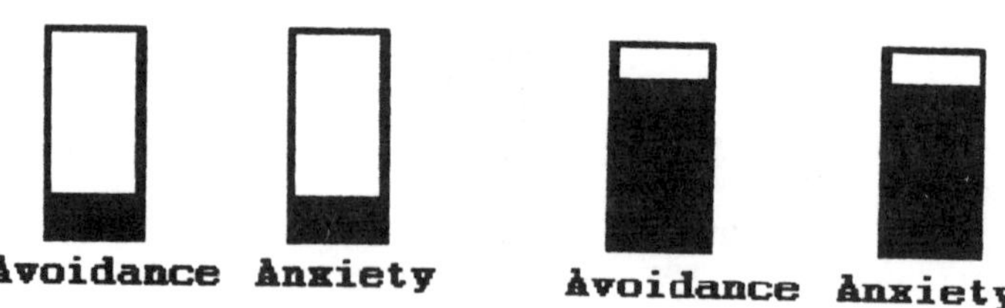

. . . the more you avoid the more anxious you become.

However, anxiety and self confidence work in reverse. The more anxious you are . . .

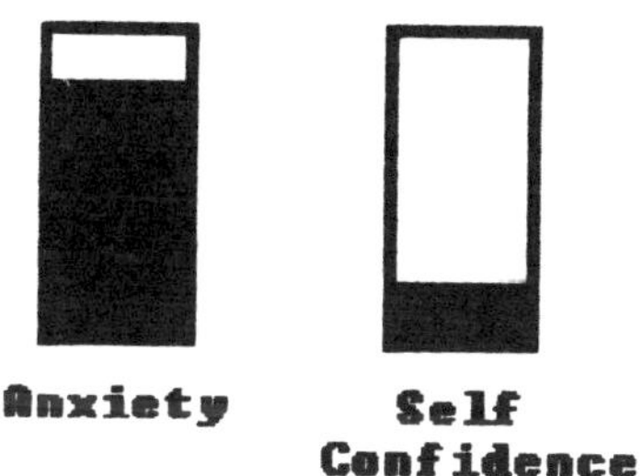

the less self confident (safe) you feel. And so . . . the less anxious you are . . .

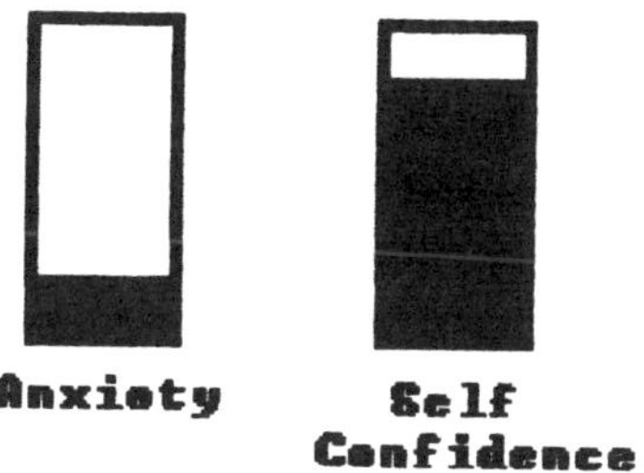

The more confident (safe) you feel.

Finally, you have this equation:

AVOIDANCE =
HIGHER ANXIETY =
LOSS OF SELF-CONFIDENCE

This is why we call avoidance, "**the crippling quick-fix.**"

Chapter 5

SELF-PROTECTION AND AVOIDANCE

By the time an individual comes to us, we know several things have already occurred. Usually, they have been seeking treatment for an extended period of time. So, if this is a similar situation for you and you're feeling frustrated and confused, that is normal. If you're feeling hopeless, that's the logical emotion one feels when they cannot solve a problem in a reasonable amount of time. The emotion that *follows* feeling hopeless for a prolonged period, is depression.

The process looks like this . . .

CONFUSION (inability to figure out a solution) =
HOPELESSNESS (there is no solution) = **DEPRESSION**

Unfortunately, when individuals seek treatment for anxiety disorders the therapist immediately recognizes the depression (because that is what therapists have been trained to recognize). Then, the therapist thinks *"I have found the problem! Obviously, if this person were not so depressed they would feel more motivated to shop, drive across town, eat in restaurants, leave the house, etc."* So, they begin to hunt for "underlying" reasons why you may be depressed.

*"Is your relationship with your spouse a good one? Maybe you're just trying to get him to help you more, so your fear of shopping forces him to do the grocery shopping? Maybe you were molested or abused as a child (if you don't remember, you might be repressing it, and we'll "**hunt**" until we find it)? Do you really like your parents (maybe that's the real reason you won't*

drive across town to see them)? Do you really want to go back to that job (maybe what you really have is a fear of success)? Did you really like to eat out (maybe you're secretly angry that your husband always picked the restaurants so you decided to refuse to go at all)?" All of these things may be true, but are they the real reasons you're avoiding these activities?

Look again at our equation. Two other emotions occurred before the depression . . .

CONFUSION ("What's happening to me? How can I stop It?") and then, HOPELESSNESS ("Nothing I do seems to help.")

It's important for anxiety sufferers to understand how they became depressed and "*immobilized.*" Why? Because it is the key to becoming more mobile and preventing it from happening again. We have never met a client who didn't have this uppermost in their mind. One client put it succinctly; *"I would pay any amount of money not to ever have another anxiety attack again*." Unfortunately, often, they already have.

In this chapter we want to explain the answer to the first part of the equation . . .
CONFUSION: "What's happening to me?" "How can I stop it?"

In the next chapter we'll give solutions to . . .
HOPELESSNESS: "Nothing I do seems to help."

"WHAT'S HAPPENING TO ME?"

Avoidance is another word for self-protection. All of our clients come to us with well developed systems of avoidance. We understand that their avoidance doesn't mean they are psychologically weak, lazy, or mentally incompetent. It means that at one time, avoidance gave them protection from anxiety and its threatening physical symptoms.

Avoidance is a natural self-protection reaction to pain. Every animal on earth uses avoidance for self-protection. Small animals run when bigger animals approach; mice hide when cats are around; deer move away from a lion entering their territory. These are all examples of using avoidance for self-protection. Each is avoiding an encounter with something they instinctively know they are not equipped to battle.

Few voluntarily enter a battle they do not expect to win. Avoidance is an attempt toward self-protection. Unfortunately, we *"win the battle, and lose the war"* when we use avoidance as a continual self-protection against anxiety attacks.

Soon this protection, *avoidance,* becomes as costly a problem as the anxiety attack itself. *"I was just trying to avoid having more anxiety, I didn't mean to give up a huge part of my life (such as driving, shopping, or going to restaurants)!"*

We have seen many different kinds of avoidances, most centering on the more traditional activities or events of; shopping, driving, parties, elevators, staying alone, or doing certain activities alone. Usually this occurs in places a person feels they cannot get out of quickly or easily, or there would be some sort of embarrassment to them if they were to actually *"lose control"*.

The following are a series of typical stories about the ways people will try to *"protect themselves"* by using avoidance. Please pay close attention to what happens *before* and *after* the first anxiety attack, as well as to the *"solutions"* they come up with to make sure they don't panic again, and . . . how much this *"solution"* eventually costs them.

DANIEL AND ELEVATORS

Daniel had been in sales for years. He had always made enough money to raise a family and put his children through school. However, recently, times had been rough. Because of the economy, he had been forced to change jobs several times. In his present job he was selling to an over-marketed clientele. Each day was a struggle to stay ahead of his competition.

On one especially trying day, Daniel had been rushed from the time he began work that morning. As he worked his way through his schedule, things seemed to go wrong at each step. *"This person wasn't in, that person was too busy to see him,"* and so on. You know how it gets some days. To top that, he missed an important appointment at noon when his secretary was unable to reach him. Yes, it was one of *those days.*

As Daniel rushed to meet his last appointment of the day, he squeezed his way into an already-crowded elevator. Immediately, as he watched the doors close, he started to feel lightheaded and wished he had waited for an elevator that was less crowded. He began to feel smothered and realized it would be several floors before the doors would open. This was going to be a very long ride.

It was unusually hot and he wanted to stop and get off. But this would be embarrassing for him to manage, so he stuck it out. His heart raced and he began to perspire profusely. *"What if the doors wouldn't open and I can't get out?",* he thought. The doors were slow to open but, finally they did open and Daniel hurried out. Relieved to be out of the close space, he wondered why he felt so strange. The elevator incident stayed *"in the back"* of his mind for the rest of the day.

The next morning, on the way to see his first client, he remembered the experience with the elevator the day before. His client was on the eleventh floor and the morning crowd had not cleared the lobby yet, and the elevators were still busy and full.

This was an important meeting to Daniel. He definitely didn't need another experience like yesterday. He watched the people getting on and off the elevators for a moment and then decided to try the stairs. He didn't need to be *"rattled"* before the first meeting of the day and the exercise would be good for him.

It was many weeks before Daniel made himself ride an elevator again. By then, his experience was worse than before. *What was he to do? Never ride another elevator? Would he have to climb stairs the rest of his life? Suppose the client was on the 50th floor . . . or the 100th!*

A few weeks later, Daniel decided that his 11th floor client was becoming a *"problem"* to fit into his schedule. Maybe he could do O.K. without him on his customer-list after all? *"I can use that time to get another client who is easier to get to,"* he reasoned.

KAREN AND LARGE STORES

Karen lived in a small city. There were lots of malls and discount stores to shop in and she always enjoyed *"bargain hunting."* One day as she was in a large department store shopping for school clothes for her children. She could sense the feeling of becoming lightheaded and dizzy. The fluorescent lights overhead seemed to get brighter and she heard a faint ringing noise that she couldn't seem to locate.

She continued to shop for a few more minutes, and thinking maybe she had too much coffee at breakfast, she remembered feeling rushed and edgy all morning. She tried to hurry, remembering she had many errands to do that day, but the feeling persisted and soon her heart began to race and she felt disoriented. Glancing for the exit where she entered the store, she couldn't remember it's location. Suddenly her vision blurred and she became scared, certain she'd be unable to find her way out of the store and would make a scene. She definitely *needed* to get out of the store. She was feeling more frightened by the second. Her heart racing and her ears ringing again, Karen finally found an exit. She felt faint and overwhelmed. She knew she had been close to passing out, and this would have embarrassed her tremendously. She would have hated calling attention to herself.

After several minutes, Karen felt more at ease and she stayed outside until she felt normal again. She was exhausted and decided she'd had enough shopping for one day.

That night she told her husband what had happened and he reassured her that it was probably something she had eaten. She was not content with that answer so her husband offered to go back with her the next evening. He must have been right, she felt fine the following evening.

It was several days before Karen needed to go back to that particular store . She was apprehensive all that morning thinking about going alone. And she worried; "*What will happen this time? What if I can't find the door fast enough and I faint or make a scene?*" She debated with herself all morning until finally deciding she would call her husband to see if he would meet her there after work, she needed his advice on a few purchases anyway. Her husband met her, they shopped, and she felt much better.

Soon, Karen decided she really didn't mind shopping with her husband. She didn't spend as much time and money with him along. She also felt it was probably good for them to spend more time together and they liked to eat out afterward, so it was a good deal "*all the way around*".

Unfortunately, Karen was starting to have similar feelings while standing in the check-out line at the grocery store. She began to worry about why she was having those same feelings, or worse, in the grocery store. She felt assured that if her husband didn't mind mall shopping, he wouldn't mind grocery shopping. Maybe it was also time her older daughter learned how to do the grocery shopping for the family. She would need to learn these household skills eventually.

TINA AND DRIVING

Tina was a busy mother of three children, all under ten years of age. She was den-mother, home-room mother, and a Sunday school teacher. Tina liked her reputation of being dependable, and so did everyone else. She was the mother to call when someone canceled and couldn't make the cupcakes or chaperon the class trip. She was always *"on the go",* with dance lessons, car pools, baseball practice, and always seemed to be in a hurry.

Tina enjoyed all her *"jobs"*, but soon realized she was sometimes stretched too thin. It seemed there were just not enough hours in the day. By the end of the day she always seemed exhausted and usually still hadn't finished. She had more than her share of aches and pains, but she told herself she would rest when the children were out of school for the summer.

One afternoon Tina picked the children up at school to take them to the dentist. Having several errands to do and being in a hurry, she decided to take the freeway to save time. As she entered the traffic, she noticed it was unusually heavy and slow moving. Impatiently, she realized she'd made the wrong choice. There was a *"traffic bottle neck"* caused by road work ahead, and already other people were jamming the exits to get off the freeway. She would be stuck until she got past the construction.

Tina thought about all the time she was wasting and began to feel trapped and anxious as she waited. She started to feel lightheaded and wished she had not taken the freeway. The longer she waited the dizzier she felt. Her hands began to tremble and her palms started to sweat. She'd probably miss the dental appointment and would have to reschedule. It would be one more thing she'd have to *"cram"* into next week and into her schedule that was already full.

Her heart began to beat rapidly. *"Would these cars ever move?"* The minutes dragged on and all her symptoms escalated; a pounding heart, trembling hands, feeling faint and unsteady. Finally, the traffic began to move. As she drove off the freeway she promised herself she would never get in that predicament again.

Shaken and confused, she drove on to the dentist office. *"You just couldn't trust freeways,"* she thought. She felt exhausted and uncomfortable for the rest of the day. Several days later she had an errand to do on the other side of town. *"It's faster to take the freeway,"* she reasoned. But, the memory of her experience was still fresh. *"What if it happened again? What if I get stuck on the freeway again? What if I faint or pass out?,"* Tina worried.

She decided it was not worth the risk, she would not save that much time anyway. *"They were always working on the freeway,"* she told herself, as she planned another route across town.

Over the next several weeks Tina decided to avoid the freeways altogether and made elaborate detours to avoid the possibility of driving on them. She changed dentists, reasoning, *"I don't have time to drive across town. I'll find a dentist that's closer."*

When her daughter needed to go to a dance recital on the other side of town, Tina decided her daughter was *"doing too much, and that she needed to put more time into her homework."* Tina was also beginning to feel uncomfortable driving down streets she was unfamiliar with. *"You never know when they might lead to a freeway,"* she said again. She also noticed, sometimes on busy streets, that her hands would tremble or her palms would sweat. This was also happening even when she was riding with her husband on the freeway.

MARIA AND RESTAURANTS

Maria worked in the secretarial pool of a large law firm. Her work was fast-paced and deadline-oriented. The lawyers consistently turned their work in late and wanted it back early. Most of the time the typing pool was understaffed and it seemed there was always a backlog of work.

One morning, as Maria worked hurriedly to finish a brief that had to be completed by 2:00 p.m., the attorney burst into her office with more last-minute revisions. She told him she couldn't finish the brief with the new changes by the time he needed it. *"But I have to have the completed copy before 2:00 p.m.,"* he told her. She promised she would complete it.

Maria knew she'd have to work through lunch and early afternoon to finish it. She typed frantically for several hours and finally, at 1:30 p.m., she completed the work. But, she was tired and hungry and realizing she had not eaten, she decided to take a break and go to the cafeteria around the corner from the office. The cafeteria was crowded and noisy. As she stood in the line she knew she wouldn't be able to relax there, but didn't have enough time to go anywhere else.

As Maria waited her turn she began to think about all the other work she had to put off to complete the attorney's brief by his deadline. It would all be waiting for her when she got back from lunch. She became impatient, and her heartbeat accelerated. The noise in the cafeteria seemed louder than usual and she felt nauseous. *"Why did I come here?"*, she asked herself. *"I'll never get all that work finished!"*

Suddenly, she became dizzy and felt like she might faint or black out. Telling herself she was just hungry did not make her feel any better. The lunch line seemed to be getting longer and the lights brighter. She began to hyperventilate and she felt as if she couldn't get enough air. *"I've **got** to get out of here!",* she told herself. Maria left her place in line and ran out of the building.

She slowly walked back to her office. She was alarmed over how she had felt. She began regaining her composure. She still felt afraid, and had no idea what had happened to her but was certain she never wanted it to happen again, whatever it was. Maria felt tense and fatigued all afternoon.

Work at the office continued as usual for the next several days. On Friday, her coworker suggested they all go to lunch to celebrate the end of a long week. Her friend mentioned eating at the cafeteria, but Maria immediately felt anxious and suggested they just get something from the office refrigerator and eat outside. Her friend agreed and Maria felt relieved. She remembered her experience earlier in the week and did not want to repeat it.

Maria enjoyed her lunch and told herself it was a better idea to eat outside anyway. She didn't return to the cafeteria for several days. Then one morning the secretaries decided they would go to lunch at a local restaurant. All morning Maria dreaded going to the restaurant, *"What if I have the same problem and faint this time? What if someone notices I'm having a problem? How will I explain it if I have to leave in the middle of lunch?"*

By noon Maria decided she was just too busy to go. The group left without her. Soon, Maria was avoiding eating out all together. *"I really don't need to be spending money eating out anyway. We see each other enough at the office, we don't need to eat together too,"* she told herself. Maria was also beginning to feel uncomfortable eating at family get-togethers.

* * *

Avoidance is a form of self protection. Because avoidance has some immediate advantages, avoiding anxiety-provoking situations frequently becomes an overworked tool. Most of our clients would prefer another tool. They are not *happy* avoiding the activities that brought them pleasure in the past.

Neither Daniel, Karen, Tina nor Maria were happy with the results of their efforts to control having anxiety attacks. Avoidance is like a snowball rolling down a hill, the more they did it, the bigger the problem became. Avoidance causes problems to spread, but until there is a "*better tool*" for self protection, people will continue to avoid. **Is there a better tool?** We have found there is . . .

Chapter 6

IT'S ALL IN THE APPROACH

It's common sense to avoid what hurts us. When an individual walks into our office, we understand they have come to us because they have exhausted their own resources for helping themselves, that somewhere along the way they began to have emotionally and physically upsetting experiences called "*anxiety attacks*."

Frightened and confused, they began to avoid the kinds of situations that seemed to trigger them. Usually they have tried unsuccessfully for a long time, not to avoid. But, without success, most of us lose motivation to continue trying. Success is necessary to any continued effort. We found that most have ceased to approach their problems altogether by the time they come to us for help.

From the time of their first anxiety attack, our clients start to develop "*approach*" problems. They see their success in very black and white terms. They will succeed and do it comfortably (riding elevators, crossing bridges, shopping, driving, staying alone, etc.) or they don't do it comfortably and fail. Usually the effort does not count and the failure has something to do with them intrinsically (I'm just weak). Obviously, these types of thought do not inspire further effort. Why are we not able to think more positively and rationally?

To understand why we think this way, it is important to go back to our anxiety scale. Refer to the anxiety scale for thoughts at Level 6 and above . . .

"I'm scared I'm not going to be able to handle this, what if I lose control?"

This type of thinking is called "**catastrophic**", and it means that your anxiety level is very high. It is impossible to think in a different, more positive manner until your anxiety level comes down. Expecting yourself to evaluate your efforts rationally when your anxiety level is high would be like expecting to see clearly in the dark.

Experiencing high levels of anxiety is like putting on a tinted pair of sunglasses. Everything you look at or evaluate becomes tinted. This is why all your efforts look and feel negative and catastrophic.

Continuous positive thinking requires concentration, and concentration is one of the first abilities hampered when your anxiety level is high. Positive thinking becomes just one more thing you can't succeed at. This is why *"positive"* thinking doesn't work when your anxiety level is high. When your anxiety level is low, positive or rational thinking works well. However, the more anxious you feel, the less control you will have over your thinking.

We tell our clients not to worry when they can't "control" their thinking. It's an impossible, frustrating task. This would be like asking them to catch greased pigs. *"Anxious thoughts, like greased pigs, are fast, slippery, and totally uncontrollable."* Ask anyone who has ever tried to change a catastrophic thought like *"I know I'm going to pass out and make a fool out of myself."*

It pops up whenever it wants to; seems to have a mind of its own, and no matter how much you try to reason it away *("But, I've never passed out before.")* it always seems to come back. So, do not pursue unattainable goals! The only way you can change your thinking is to **lower your anxiety level.**

When your thinking becomes catastrophic or very negative, *("I just know I'll never do this!")* understand this is because you are experiencing a very high level of anxiety. If changing your thoughts is impossible, then what will lower your anxiety level?

"IT'S EASIER TO ACT YOUR WAY INTO A NEW WAY OF THINKING, THAN TO THINK YOUR WAY INTO A NEW WAY OF ACTING."

We have already discussed how *"avoiding"* can raise your general anxiety level and move you closer to another anxiety attack. Therefore, it is obvious that *"approaching"* would lower your general anxiety level, right? Yes, it would, but it has to be accomplished carefully.

Already you're thinking *"But I tried riding elevators, going shopping and driving on a busy streets many times. But, my anxiety level just kept going up and up, until finally I had to stop trying."* Please remember, we use the word *"approach"*. . . not *"do."* Usually, anxious people miss this distinction. *"Approaching"* is an entirely different way of doing things.

Do you remember when you learned to drive? Your parents probably didn't take you out on a major freeway to learn. How did they teach you? Chances are they spent much time in helping you build your confidence (and probably theirs) by having you go through what we call *"approach behaviors."*

They also, undoubtedly, never let you tackle busy streets until you could drive empty ones first. Do you remember after driving those empty streets repeatedly, how bored you felt? *"I'm ready for the big stuff,"* you thought. All of these *"approaches"* built your confidence to the point where you were ready for more difficult things. Without those *"approaches"* your confidence (or your ability) would not have been there.

Successful "approaching" accomplishes two things:

1. It lowers your general anxiety level. When your level is lowered, your thinking becomes less catastrophic. Look at the difference between the thinking between a Level 5 and a Level 7 (Refer to the anxiety scale in Chapter 3 for the thinking characteristics at Levels 5 and 7).

2. Creates a more positive evaluation of what you attempted and therefore more optimism (and motivation) about trying again. Remember, without success it's difficult to keep trying.

Built into each step must be the certainty, not just the opportunity, for success:

You must be asking, "*So how do I successfully approach something I have been avoiding?* We learn how to do most things in a step-by-step manner. Built into each step should be the certainty, not just the opportunity, for success. This is true for *"re-learning"* also. "Re-learning" is what people have to do when, because of anxiety, they have begun to avoid some activity. They must learn, or re-learn, to do it comfortably again. However, remember that the main goal for re-learning is to **lower your general anxiety level.** The competency you wish for in a particular area will come, but feeling emotionally and physically more comfortable is the first result you will experience. In the next chapter we'll go back to the client cases we cited in Chapter 4, (Daniel and elevators, Karen and large stores, Tina and driving, and Maria with her trouble in restaurants) and give a detailed summary of how we structured therapy for each.

We believe the following conditions were essential in each of their treatment.

a. They had accepted that their problem was a psychological problem and not a physical problem. Anxiety attacks are an anxiety disorder. High levels of anxiety can cause many painful physical symptoms. But having physical symptoms (ringing in the ears, dizziness, heart palpitations, etc.) does not mean you have a brain tumor, inner ear disease or are going to have a heart attack. Usually people who, after several medical examinations, are still going to physicians looking for physical reason for their symptoms, are also looking for a "quick fix" for their problems or more reasons to continue to avoid.

b. They were no longer willing to accept their restrictions. Some people are comfortable with their restrictions. They don't live near freeways, so freeways are not a problem. They work in a two-story building and don't need to ride elevators, so there's no problem with an elevator being crowded or with climbing stairs.

Others don't mind having their husband (or wife) drive and shop with them. These people are **not** good candidates for field work, since they can afford to accept their restriction.

Good candidates for field work can't afford their restriction. Their office has moved to an 20-story building, they live in a city that if you can't drive freeways, it takes all day to get to where you're going and they have to be able to drive and shop and eat out. They don't have the time nor the desire to wait around for their spouse or *"safety person"* to take them places.

We have found that with these two elements, anyone can recover from anxiety attacks.

Field Work

We call our treatment method *"field work"*, because we work with our clients in the field, in places where they have anxiety attacks; in malls, grocery stores, elevators, restaurants, freeways etc. We've found that to eliminate anxiety attacks you have to work on becoming comfortable in areas where the anxiety attacks occur. Just as you can't learn to cook an exotic meal without being in the kitchen, you simply cannot learn to successfully approach areas of avoidance without being there and experiencing it, on site.

Most people we've worked with have tried to conquer their areas of avoidance without success. If they could comfortably approach these areas, they would have no problem. What we are proposing is not a new idea for you, but our methods of how to "*structure the approach process*" will be new and more helpful.

Premises of Field Work

In doing field work, remember the goal is to reduce your anxiety not to just complete a task. Field work is based on the following premises.

1. Anxiety attacks are caused by an overflow of anxiety.

2. The anxiety overflow is usually displaced onto an object, situation, or person that becomes the focus of one's general anxiety.

3. Avoidance of the object, situation or person increases one's general anxiety which in turn increases the amount of anxiety being displaced.

4. Reducing the anxiety displaced onto an object, situation or person, in turn, reduces general anxiety.

Tools That Make It Work

We've also developed some terms that we will explain in this chapter, to help you structure your field work for success. These terms are: **Small Step by Small Step, Repetition, White Knuckling, Jumping in the Deep End, Distraction and Choice Practice.**

We have found that most anxious people approach their areas of avoidance by ***Jumping In The Deep End*** (take too large a step) of an activity and try to ***White Knuckle*** (anxiety level above 6) through the experience. Many think if you **White**

Knuckle a situation enough that you will eventually get comfortable with it. **This is not true!** White Knuckling only keeps you sensitized to an activity, and thus increases your desire to avoid it.

By understanding these terms of field work you can prevent yourself from going through White Knuckling experiences that hinder progress.

Small Step by Small Step

Big Results Come In Small Packages

This principle is the backbone of field work, and the most frequently misused. People who are anxious want to be **un**-anxious, *yesterday!* **Field work is not a slow process, but it starts slow.** We break down any goal into many smaller steps. We don't ask people who have anxiety attacks while driving to begin by driving in heavy traffic. They begin by driving around the parking lot many times. We don't ask people who have anxiety in the elevator to ride to the 14th floor, and we don't ask people who have anxiety attacks while shopping in large stores to begin by actually shopping. First, they must get comfortable "*being*" in the store, without the pressure of actually having to buy. We might start with them walking around in the store for two minutes at a time, and so on . . .

When you are anxious you are impatient and frequently don't want to do the small beginning steps. *"But I need to do shopping for the whole week!"* You lack the problem-solving skills you have when your anxiety level is low. *"I don't have time to just wander around getting comfortable first!"*

However, it is important to remember how often your parents only allowed you to sit in the car behind the wheel before they allowed you to drive down the street. We always encounter opposition to this *"kid's stuff"* way of approaching problem areas. But isn't it so that our fears make scared children out of the biggest and bravest of us? Your parents took care of your natural fear of driving a big powerful engine by breaking down the skill into steps they knew you could handle.

Again, the "**small step by small step**" practice insures that you will have success with every effort. Successful efforts will bring good feelings about yourself and this keeps you practicing. If you don't have the motivation to continue it is because your steps have not been small enough.

Repetition

You Can't be Bored and Anxious at the Same Time

Often, people will practice and have success with their efforts. However, they will neglect to *"reinforce"* that success with the continuous practice that brings down their anxiety level significantly. And bringing down your anxiety level is *"what its all about"*. Many anxious people don't want to repeatedly practice a step. This is why it is important for some people to have a *"helper"* or therapist, to make sure they do the repetitive practice that insures a lower anxiety level.

How much repetition is necessary? A **lot**! How much is "a lot"? You must practice each step until you are bored with it. Yes, **bored!** Most people generally want to jump ahead after the first time they can do something comfortably. *"Wow! I felt O.K. that time"*, they say. *"Can we go to the next step now?"*

But we know that particular success is not really "theirs" yet. And it will not be, until they can do it without thinking about it. This is why we ask that you repeat the step until you become bored with doing it. Boredom means it is no longer a challenge. And when something is no longer a challenge, you cease to think about what you are doing. Your mind wanders naturally, and you focus on other things in your environment. You might think about what you're going to have for dinner, what your children are doing after school, are your clothes clean for tomorrow, or other routine day-to-day concerns.

In other words, the normal things you think about when your level is low and you're not worried about your physical safety. Have you ever noticed how your mind will wander when you're bored? And boredom with what you're doing will bring this "*normal*" thinking. We know it's difficult for most to imagine that they could be "bored" with something they fear so much. But, continuous repetition acts like a wet blanket on your anxiety and will cool it down considerably. It amazes our clients how well this principle works.

White Knuckling

Forcing It Doesn't Work

By this time a few of you are saying, "But I tried repetitive practice and it never got boring. It never became easier." Let us explain what you were doing wrong. When practice doesn't bring your anxiety down, you are practicing at **a step that is too difficult for you.** When you are practicing at a continuous high level of anxiety we call this "*white knuckling.*" When you are "*white knuckling*" a step, it will never get easier. Anytime you are continuously practicing at a level above 6, you're white knuckling.

Practice at a level under 6. When you're at Level 6, it means you're slightly uncomfortable, feeling a few physical symptoms, but not overwhelmed by them. (Refer to the anxiety scale for the list of symptoms at each level.) Never "white knuckle" your practice or field work. By doing this, you will only be "*reinforcing*" the idea that you'll never do this comfortably again.

Jumping In the Deep End

A Big Hurt that Doesn't Help

If you're trying to teach a child to multiply, you don't start by giving them multiplication problems, you would teach them the multiplication tables first, right? It wouldn't matter how often they attempted to do the problems, if the foundation isn't there, they will never solve them. Practicing something that is anxiety-producing for you works on the same principle. You've jumped past several steps if your repetitive practice does not bring your level down. You're trying multiplication problems before you have learned your tables. Slow down and go back to an easier step, or break down the step you're attempting into smaller parts.

Often, someone will not have the patience to go back to the "beginning," but it's important to their success to start from where they can do something comfortably and work their way **up** instead of starting over their head. Remember, each step must hold the *certainty,* not just *potential,* for success. You cannot *"make"* yourself do things more comfortably. **Forcing it will only make your anxiety level go up.**

When we see someone *"jumping in the deep end"* it means they feel really bad about being disabled. They feel that it is silly to be having this problem. They feel anxious and afraid and want to be out of this pickle before anyone finds out. So they ignore the first ten reasonable steps and say, *"There! I should be able to start on step eleven. I'm a smart person. I see how this step-by-step process works!"*

They forget that anxiety is not a logical process, and although you may clearly *"understand,"* ***"doing"*** is another matter altogether. In our examples you will see how we handle a situation where someone has been "jumping in the deep end" hoping if they just do it enough times, eventually it will get easier.

Distraction
A Mini-Vacation From Anxiety

This is one of the more common techniques we use in field work. Many people are already using this technique to lower their anxiety level. When they come to us, we teach them how to get even more *"mileage"* out of it. We practically guide them away from *"anxious thinking."*

Anxious thinking means that you are focusing almost exclusively on your body and you are negatively *"predicting."* When someone is anxious, their attention span is very short. They are totally focused on their body, hoping to protect themselves from another emotional overflow or anxiety attack.

When we are working in the field with a client we keep a stack of magazines, similar to the National Enquirer or Woman's World, on hand. If someone's anxiety level should escalate, we have them halt practicing and read for a few minutes. The reading material has to be of a certain kind, the articles must be short and interesting. A book will not do. High levels of anxiety take away the ability to concentrate, thus short articles, with no more than a few paragraphs, are necessary. A book or technical magazine will only be more frustrating, because your attention span is short, and will drive your anxiety level higher (*"I can't even concentrate anymore!").* This distraction away from your "anxious" thinking will bring your level down. (Some recommend snapping a rubber band on your arm or counting backwards as distraction methods. Our experience is that "rubber band" snapping or counting backward is not engaging enough to distract someone from anxiously focusing on their physical symptoms.)

In the beginning, you may have to read for several minutes (sometimes as long as fifteen) before your level will decline. But, it will go down; it always does. Never go back to practice until your level is down to a 5 or less. You'll be *"white knuckling"* if you do.

Choice Practice

Anticipatory Anxiety Reducer

Choice practice is the key to lowering your general anxiety level. Have you ever watched a child learn to play a new sport? They might go to lessons you pay for, **but they will not reap any real benefits until they practice** *"on their own."* The same is true with therapy and practice. **You can pay for therapy, but you won't reap the real benefits** (lower general anxiety level, fewer physical symptoms, more feelings of being in control) **until you** ***"choice practice."*** Choice practice means practice you do for "*practice's* sake."

For example, after we've had a few sessions with a client we give them homework to do between sessions. If the homework is *"going to the store and buying one item,"* occasionally some will not go and say, "Well, we just didn't need anything." Or if the homework is driving three blocks from home, they will wait until its time to do another necessary errand and call that homework.

Choice practice means efforts you make *"when you don't have to."* You might ask, *"What's the difference? I'm still doing it!"* The difference is enormous. **Doing something when the only reason you do it is to practice, means it is individually important to you.** It reduces your anticipatory anxiety when you practice something that will benefit you, rather than just run errands. Choice practice builds your emotional strength and self-confidence. And the higher your self-confidence in your skills, the lower will be your general anxiety. Anxiety and self-confidence work in reverse. The stronger your feelings of self-confidence, the less anxious you feel.

A reminder: You can't *"think"* (affirmations, positive self talk, rational thinking, etc.) your way into feelings of self-confidence. This is like hoping to win the lottery without buying a ticket. Self-confidence is based on your skills that you can successfully **do** something. You have to *"do"* (through choice practice) your way into them.

Sound impossible? Not at all, **if** you structure steps appropriately and choice practice on your own.

A little more about choice practice. Doing something because it's *"convenient"* or not doing it because you can't come up with a good reason or you can't find the time (*"We just didn't need anything at the store yesterday" or "I waited to practice driving until I had to go pick up my daughter")* might mean your practice step is too large. Break the step down more.

Separation Anxiety

It's also important to point out that some people will need to be working on two areas of avoidance with their field work. One area, is their avoidance of an activity or situation like avoidance of large stores, but they will also need to work on their avoidance of doing these activities without a *"safety person"* or *"safety kit."* The "safety kit" can be anything you take with you that makes you feel more secure. This can be a water bottle, gum, car, rubber bands, beer, rabbits foot, medication, etc. Usually it is *"safety person" or "safety kit"* of medication.

To do field work successfully you must work on both of these issues. This means you need to *gradually* develop more distance away from the *"safety person" or "safety kit".* Dealing with your separation anxiety from your "safety person" or "safety kit" is accomplished in the same way that you deal with your primary area of avoidance . . . **SMALL STEP BY SMALL STEP.** Those people who are house-bound need to practice gaining more walking distance from their house and from their *"safety person"*. Those with *"safety kits"* need to start on field work steps they feel comfortable doing without their "safety kits". If you are working in stores, start by leaving the "safety kit" in the car, or let your "helper" keep them for you while you practice.

For those who are taking medication, it is advisable to keep your dosage stable while you are practicing field work. You are still avoiding if you double up on medication while practicing. This only increases your dependency on medication, and does not decrease your anxiety. For those who want to stop taking medication, it is best to keep your dosage stable while doing field work, until you feel confident enough to get off the medication. Always consult your physician before you change your dosage.

Field Work "Helper"

Some of you will be able to do field work on your own. Others will need a "helper" or will need professional help. A good "*rule of thumb*" for needing help is usually based on your degree of restriction. Those who have a low degree of restriction, where you are only avoiding one area such as elevators, bridges or large stores, could try field work on their own. Those who have more than one area of restriction will probably need a "helper" or a therapist for their field work.

The role of "helper" is to hold you back and keep you from taking too large a step. The helper can also help you **Distract** so you can reduce your anxiety when it goes up. **Make sure if you work with a "helper" that you also practice on your own,** so that you can learn to perform the step without a *"safety person"*. Practice new steps with a "helper" and then **Choice Practice** the same steps without your "helper".

Review

All of these elements are important to successful field work. It is important for you to understand how avoidance restricts your lifestyle and increases your general anxiety which is why we call it *"the crippling quick fix,"* also how "field work" can lower your general anxiety level, and build your self-confidence. After all, if you don't know what a *"weed"* (avoidance) looks like, you can't pull it out, can you?

What if you are uncomfortable in more than one area? This is not uncommon. However, **you should pick one area to work on, the one most important to you and the easiest one for you to practice regularly.** The other areas will get easier for you as you improve in the chosen problem. Remember, when your general level comes down through successful step by step practice, you will take this reduced level into everything you do.

Let's go on to Chapter 7 and look at our client stories again. We'll take you through each case in a detailed summary and show you how "field work" lowered their general anxiety level and gave them back control of activities they were having to avoid. Watch closely how, before each client masters the area they are working on, they begin to see the benefits of their general anxiety level going down in other areas of their life. They begin to sleep better, they experience less depression, they reported having less physical symptoms, but the most important difference is, **they feel back in control of their life.**

Chapter 7

FIELD WORK

"It's easier to act your way into a new way of thinking, than to think your way into a new way of acting."

If avoidance is a, *"quick fix"* and will eventually do more damage than good, then what is the answer? In order to provide an answer, we'll have to go back to our client stories. We would like for you to see how *"practical approaching"* works in a real situation, one that may be similar to your own.

Before we begin field work, we discuss with our clients guidelines we believe are important to their success in treatment. These are the goals of field work and important points you need to remember. These are also good guidelines for evaluating any kind of therapy you are seeking for eliminating your anxiety attacks.

Guidelines for Field Work

1. Field work has practical steps and objectives. It is easy to understand, and structured so you will never have to experience another anxiety attack. With properly structured steps you should not have another anxiety attack. Field work does not teach how to *"cope" or "accept"* anxiety attacks, but how to eliminate them. The purpose of treatment is to reduce your anxiety. Field work for anxiety attacks is brief, but is accomplished in a **Small Step by Small Step** manner.

2. In field work, the client's anxiety directs the therapy. In field work the size of a step and the time spent on a step is determined by your anxiety level. You should be able to perform the step at a comfortable level before moving to the next step. It is more important to be bored with the step rather than going to the next step prematurely. Your goal is to lower your general anxiety, not to quickly move through the steps. In field work the anxiety you experience for a step is very important feedback for you and should not be denied.

3. Field work focuses on *"approaching" not "thinking."* Therapy that focuses on how to change your thinking doesn't understand how much avoidance influences thinking or how quickly approaching clears up anxious thinking. When your anxiety level is so high that you are "spilling over" with anxiety attacks, it is impossible to control your thinking.

Anxiety is not a *"rational"* process, it is an *"emotional"* process. Any effort to think or reason your way out of your anxiety attacks will only be frustrating and depressing for you. It is more important to break down your approach step to something you are comfortable with, than to spend time trying to approach the whole task rationally (by changing your thinking).

4. Field work focuses on lowering your general anxiety level, not just completing a feared task. The primary goal of field work is not just to overcome a feared task, it is to reduce your general anxiety to a level where you are not "spilling over" with anxiety attacks. Being able to overcome the feared task is a result of lowering your general anxiety. Since, as avoidance increases, anxiety increases, when you begin to "*approach*" instead of *"avoid"* and do it successfully (comfortably) your general anxiety level will decrease rapidly.

As your anxiety decreases you also quickly regain your competency in these specific areas. After approximately ten sessions of field work, you should sleep with greater ease and comfort, have less aches and pains, and have less anxiety-related symptoms such as headaches and stomach pain. You will also feel less depressed and more emotionally competent.

5. Field work needs to be practiced at least three times a week. Anticipatory anxiety is a major barrier to successful treatment. The best method for dealing with anticipatory anxiety is to not give it time to build up. By practicing several days in a week you can keep your anticipatory anxiety at a manageable level. The more days in the week you practice, the easier the practice will be and the quicker your anxiety will decrease. Try not to go several days without practicing. When you skip days between practice you build up a greater amount of anticipatory anxiety and it takes longer to reduce your anxiety level again.

We'll now go back to our client stories, remember our list of therapeutic terms:

FIELD WORK
SMALL STEP BY SMALL STEP
REPETITION
WHITE KNUCKLING
JUMPING IN THE DEEP END
DISTRACTION
CHOICE PRACTICE

DANIEL'S FIELD WORK

Daniel's general anxiety level had been steadily escalating for several years. With children in high school, the recession, a more competitive job market, and several job changes in a row, Daniel's anxiety level was very high on a daily basis. He was a prime candidate for an unexpected anxiety attack.

When we began to work with him, he was only riding elevators when he couldn't avoid it. If he was with a client he'd force himself to ride the elevator. On all other occasions he took the stairs.

We had our initial session with Daniel and explained how his avoidance was continuing his anxiety attacks. We worked out a schedule and made a plan to meet three times a week **(Field Work)** at a local twenty-story building that had several elevators. The building had minimal traffic and very few people using the elevators, so it was ours exclusively most of the time.

On the first session Daniel's anxiety level was a 7 as we began the session. He was sure, we wanted him to *"just get in the elevator and ride",* something he had tried himself with disastrous results (**Jumping In The Deep End)**. We explained to him again that the goal of field work was to reduce anxiety, not learn to cope with anxiety attacks. We explained to him that until he could sit on the bench next to the elevator comfortably, we wouldn't ask him to go to the next step (**Small Step By Small Step**).

For the first session we sat and talked next to the elevator (**Repetition)** while watching other people come and go on the elevators. Daniel told us it was frustrating for him to see others ride the elevators so easily and without thought, when it was so difficult for him.

On the 2nd session, Daniel said that although he was anxious as he came in the building to meet us, his level was now down to a 5 sitting next to the elevator. A Level 5 is the level we look for before we go on to the next step. If the level does not come down within a reasonable time (20 minutes) the step is too big and needs to be broken down further. With the proper step, anxiety **will** come down.

We practice patience while we are waiting, and read magazines and talk **(Distraction**). The next step was for Daniel to walk in and out of the elevator. **(Small Step By Small Step)** until he could do it at a Level 5 **(Repetition)**. It took Daniel five times **(Repetition**) of walking in and out of the elevator before he felt comfortable.

After the first two times Daniel reported that he had

fleeting thoughts, *"that the elevator would take off with him trapped in it."* We saw his catastrophic thinking as an indication that Daniel's anxiety level was elevated (over a 6) and that it was time for him to take a break. We did not try to talk him out of this kind of thinking, but we could help him control how often he had catastrophic thoughts by slowing down his practice and taking breaks.

After about seven trials (**Repetition**) he wanted to try riding a **few** floors **(Jumping In The Deep End**). Again we told him he was jumping ahead. The next step would be for him to ride up only one floor and walk back down **(Small Step By Small Step**). We spent the rest of the session with Daniel mastering going up one floor (**Repetition**).

We decided this would be the step that Daniel would need to *"over learn"* or practice until he was "bored" **(Repetition**). So we combined many breaks with reading to lower his anxiety level **(Distraction**) and made sure he became thoroughly bored (**Repetition**) and competent in riding one floor.

After the 3rd session we gave Daniel his first homework assignment **(Choice Practice**). Between each session he was instructed to practice riding the elevator up one floor. We emphasized that he not do more, and **particularly he should not practice steps he has not previously practiced in our sessions.** He was to bring a newspaper to read **(Distraction**) if his anxiety started to go up. He told us that his level was a 6 when he began the homework, but it went down to a 3 by the end.

At the beginning of the fifth session Daniel reported to us that his general anxiety level was decreasing. He still had all the same problems he had when he started therapy, but he seemed to not "*get so uptight*" about problems now. We explained to him that by successful approaching his problem and not avoiding, his feelings of emotional strength were increasing as his anxiety level was decreasing.

Daniel was surprised and delighted with this side benefit

of increased self-esteem. We pointed out that **self-esteem increases as you successfully approach your fear.** He didn't have to wait until he totally mastered elevators before he began to feel better. During the fifth, sixth, seventh and eighth sessions Daniel practiced going to higher floors. And after the fifth session his homework included riding the elevators to the floor we had practiced during the previous session **(Choice Practice**). By the ninth session Daniel had mastered all twenty floors in the building.

During practice, if Daniel reported he was having to **White Knuckle** a step, we would have him stop and read **(Distraction**) to get his anxiety down, and then break the step down to a more comfortable level. It's always important to keep the anxiety level below a 6 or you will be **White Knuckling** the step and keeping your anxiety up.

* **Remember no matter how many times you "White Knuckle" a step, it will not get more comfortable.**

On the tenth, eleventh and twelfth session we went to other elevators. Daniel practiced in crowded ones, glass ones, small ones, slow ones, noisy ones, and ones that took an extended time for the doors to open. By this time Daniel was riding any elevator on his own comfortably. His general anxiety was significantly lower, and he had not had an anxiety attack since starting therapy. Daniel also noticed that his lower anxiety level had transferred to other areas. He felt more comfortable in crowds and felt more self-confident doing other activities on his own.

KAREN'S FIELD WORK

When Karen came to us, she was having anxiety attacks every time she shopped in large stores, alone. Sometimes she could shop with someone, but recently she was having anxiety attacks even with someone along.

In our first session she explained to us she had even

been to the emergency room twice, certain she was going to have a heart attack. Finally an E.R. doctor told her she was having anxiety attacks and although she felt reassured she wasn't going to die, she still could not go shopping alone.

She had also been to a therapist with whom she had discussed her feelings of depression and low self-esteem related to her inability to go shopping. The sessions had been informative and insightful about her childhood but had not helped her feel comfortable shopping again or make her feel less anxious.

Karen was frustrated and feeling hopeless that she would never be normal again. We began by explaining about how anxiety attacks start and how avoidance is a natural "*self protection*" reaction, but that it increases one's general anxiety. We explained field work and our treatment goals and why we didn't expect her to be able to tackle this problem on her own. We explained that our treatment would revolve around going to large stores with her to help her re-learn how to shop again comfortably (**Field Work**).

We decided to work in a medium-sized store she was already familiar with and made plans to meet three times a week for the next few weeks. She agreed, but said she became anxious even "*thinking*" about it. We assured her we would meet in *front* of the store, and that we didn't expect her to go *in* the store in the beginning **(Small Step By Small Step**).

We emphasized that we would not ask her to do anything she was uncomfortable doing **(Jumping In The Deep End**). She would only be practicing very small tasks at a time **(Small Step By Small Step**) and she had total control over how much she wanted to do.

The first day we met at the store, which had benches outside for us to sit on, Karen said her level was a 7 **(White Knuckling)**. So we backed up a step and sat in her car, in "*front*" of the store. We sat and talked for fifteen minutes and her level came down slowly. I asked her to read for a few minutes

(Distraction).

When she told us her anxiety level was at a 5, I asked her to walk to the bench and to sit and read for five minutes **(Small Step By Small Step and Distraction)**. Karen came back and reported that her level was *still* a 5. It had gone up a little but quickly came back down.

At this level Karen was only experiencing a few physical symptoms (cold hands). She wanted to know if I wanted her to go in and shop now (**Jumping In The Deep End**). We said she had several sessions in front of her before she started to shop. Our first goal would be to just get her *"comfortable"* being inside the store again. Shopping would come later **(Small Step By Small Step**), but for this session we would just get comfortable outside sitting on the bench **(Repetition)**.

The next session Karen reported her anxiety level was higher just anticipating the session. She was having a hard time remembering we weren't going to make her **Jump In The Deep End**. We explained that as long as her general anxiety level was high (6 or above), she would have catastrophic thinking about the sessions, but when her general level began to come down, her thinking would not be so *"anxious"*.

We sat on the bench and talked and read **(Distraction**), but today it took less time for Karen's level to come down to a Level 5; only fifteen minutes. This session we asked Karen if she could go in the store and stay for two minutes. She was to stay in the front of the store next to the entrance and look at anything she found interesting (**Distraction**). She agreed she would try, and we told her to come out any time her anxiety level went above a 6.

Karen went in for two minutes, came out and reported her level was the same, a 5. The next task was to stay in the store for four minutes **(Small Step By Small Step**). She went in and came out and reported this was a little more difficult, that she had been ready to come out after three minutes. We then advised her to stop and read for ten minutes **(Distraction**) and she reported her level went back to a 5. She then went back in several more times for 3 minutes. Each time it became easier **(Repetition**). When Karen was able to stay in the store for 3 minutes consistently at a Level 5, we moved to the next step.

We make a practice of starting every session with the last step we worked on in the session before. We never start a session with a new or more difficult step. So, after several practices from prior sessions in the 3rd session, we asked Karen to go in for 10 minutes and she did fine (at a Level 5). For the next three practices she continued to moving further back into the store, away from the entrance **(Small Step By Small Step**).

She had no trouble the first several tries until unexpectedly her anxiety level went up. She felt a little lightheaded and the lights in the store seemed brighter. She said she began to worry about passing out in the store. She came out and reported she had tried to stay in for the whole 10 minutes but she finally had to come out **(White Knuckling**).

We explained to her again that she was not to stay in if her level went over a 6. This should be an indication to her that she was reaching her "*tolerance level*". Staying in longer would only make her feel worse **(White Knuckling**).

We knew that the catastrophic thinking (her concern about fainting) and physical symptoms meant that her level had escalated. Karen had reached her tolerance for staying in the store, so we had her sit and read for ten minutes **(Distraction**) and her level came down again. Then she went back in for five minutes. When she came out, her level was low and she went **back in** for ten minutes again **(Repetition**). This time her level remained low and she had no thoughts about fainting.

Again, catastrophic thinking is only an indication that one's anxiety level is escalating. We understand that we cannot reason it away, nor can they. When one is very anxious and feels they might faint, they are not able to "*convince*" themselves they will not faint. In field work catastrophic thinking is only an indicator that its time for a break to reduce the anxiety level before returning to the step. It can also mean that the step is too big and needs to be broken down into smaller steps.

We stopped the session here because Karen had regained the success she started with at the inception of the session. This was a good lesson for Karen. She admitted to us if she had been alone, she would have become very discouraged and would have thought she was not making progress. Instead, she learned she could always regain her ground after a small relapse.

At the beginning of the next session, Karen reported that her general anxiety level was coming down. She was not having headaches and she was sleeping better. On the fifth and sixth session Karen worked on her length of time in the store, steadily increasing it until she was staying fifteen to twenty minutes at a time (**Small Step By Small Step**).

She began her homework at this time. She was to go to a store in her neighborhood once a day and just walk around and look (**Choice Practice**). She was instructed not to buy at this point, but to go alone.

Sessions seven through nine were spent increasing her distance away from the entrance as well as the time she remained in the store (**Small Step By Small Step**). She also practiced buying a few items. We told her to choose short check-out lines at first and then practice getting in longer lines. Her homework included buying items in the store on her own. Again, she was told not to practice during homework what she had not practiced during a session.

At the beginning of the tenth session, Karen reported she had gone to the grocery store the night before. She was able to buy most of the weeks groceries without feeling physical symptoms of anxiety or catastrophic thinking. This was the first time in over a year that she'd been able to shop comfortably and she was very happy with her success. We were also happy for Karen. We had promised Karen **that the skills she had been**

working on in one store would transfer to other stores and here was the proof.

The last four sessions with Karen were spent going to the large department store where she had experienced her first anxiety attack. Her anticipatory anxiety was high the first session but by the time she had spent the next two sessions there, she was having no problem at all. The last session she called to say she wanted to go by herself! She agreed to call us when she got home to tell us how she had done. Several hours later she called to report she had no problems and she was a very happy shopper again.

In follow-up calls from Karen one year and two years later, she told us that she can't believe she had ever been anxious about shopping. She happily informed us that when she has a stressful day, going shopping helped her to relax.

TINA'S FIELD WORK

Tina had been avoiding driving on freeways or in heavy traffic for over two years when she came to us for treatment. She said she called because, now that her oldest daughter was in junior high, she worried about the effect her anxiety was having on her children. She noticed that her daughter was starting to get uncomfortable when she was riding with someone other than Tina. Tina knew that her daughter had "*watched*" her nervousness and was displaying some of the same symptoms. Tina did not want to be an "*anxious*" role model for her children. She decided, although it would be hard, that she needed to work on becoming fully mobile again.

Tina had been on an anti-depressant for over eighteen months, upon the advice of her family physician. The medication had not helped her anxiety about driving, but it did elevate her mood some. She wanted to get off the medication because it made her mouth feel dry. But her physician informed her that her anxiety attacks would increase if she stopped taking the medication. Tina also reported she had a *"safety kit"* of tranquilizers that several different physicians had given her over the last two years.

She carried this *"safety kit"* with her wherever she went, but rarely took any of its contents. In fact, although she hadn't taken a tranquilizer in six months, all she needed to do was "*think*" about leaving the house without them to bring on an anxiety attack.

Tina had used avoidance as her main tool for dealing with anxiety attacks. She made sure she did not drive between 7:30 a.m. and 9:00 a.m. or between 4:00 p.m. and 6:30 p.m. on any day (*"I might get into heavy traffic"*), and she usually took the *"back streets"* when she did drive (*"It may take me an hour longer, but I can get to most places I want to go").*

Now, Tina was ready to take control of her life again. She wanted to stop driving back streets, and wanted to stop carrying a "safety kit" of medication. She wanted to do normal everyday activities. We explained, in our first session with Tina, how her efforts to help herself, through avoiding areas that seemed to make her anxious, had actually been increasing the possibility that she would have another anxiety attack.

We told her the best way to make sure she would never have another attack was through *"successful approaching"*. We would help her do that with field work. We said we needed to teach her to drive again comfortably. She asked if this could be done through *"relaxation techniques?"*

We explained that although relaxation and visualization techniques worked well when one's anxiety level is low (below a 5), it works very poorly when one's anxiety is at **anxiety attack levels.** We also explained that relaxation's focus on muscle relaxation could cause a person who is *"cueing off"* physical symptoms, to experience anxiety attacks. We further advised that if she was already practicing relaxation techniques and felt comfortable with them, to continue, but that it was not a requirement of field work.

A first session was arranged at a place near her home, at a time of day when she was able to drive somewhat comfortably. Tina's anxiety level was very high on the first session. She reported having an anxiety attack the night before the session when she tried to drive on a busy street near her home **(Jumping In The Deep End)**. She convinced herself that it was only a matter of *"will power"* and perhaps she had just not been trying hard enough.

Our suggestion was that she not practice on her own until she had accomplished several successful steps with us first **(Small Step By Small Step**). We didn't have to ask twice. We also explained that she did not have a "will power" problem, she had an anxiety disorder, and anxiety is fueled by avoidance, not by *"weak thinking"*.

Tina had been avoiding driving without her "*safety kit*" of medication. The first thing we asked her to do was to let us keep her kit while she practiced with us, and she could keep it with her at all other times **(Small Step By Small Step)**. She agreed, and we reassured her she could have it back anytime she wanted. As we expected, Tina could not go far without her kit, so we only asked her to go around the block **(Small Step By Small Step**). Even this was difficult for Tina. She had not realized how dependent she had become on merely having her medication in her purse. *"But I never take it!"* was her reply. We explained that a *"safety kit"* doesn't have to be **used** to become a crutch.

We followed Tina around the block in our car. She said this was easier for her. She did this at a 6 the first time and after several trips (**Repetition**) her level went down to a 5. Tina decided she wanted to try going around the block alone. It took several trips to reduce her level down to a steady 5, without us behind her (**Repetition**). We worked on this the entire first session. At the end of the session we gave her "safety kit" back to her. We told her we would take it at the beginning of each session and give it back at the end.

The next session we continued to work on the distance she could travel without her kit. We worked on driving two blocks, first following her, and when her level was a 5, she would do it alone (**Small Step By Small Step**). She accomplished three blocks in this session.

The next session we had Tina practice making a short turn into some heavier traffic, then turning around and returning to us (**Small Step By Small Step**). This was the first traffic Tina encountered, and she practiced this small segment over and over for the next two sessions (**Repetition**).

The first time around we followed her and then she practiced on her own. Any time Tina would come back to us and say, "*I felt like the cars were coming to close to me and I might get hit*," we knew that her catastrophic thinking meant her anxiety level was escalating and she needed a break. So Tina would stop and read until her level came down (**Distraction**), even if it took twenty minutes. We never practiced until her level was a 5 again. Practicing at high levels of anxiety would only convince her that this was difficult and frightening. Finally, she was driving the segment at a 5 consistently, and we added another block where there was heavier traffic.

Because Tina was motivated, we began giving her homework at this point (**Choice Practice**). Twice a week we asked her to practice, without her "safety kit", driving the two block stretch where there was heavier traffic. She was not to do any more, even if she felt she could. Tina's tendency would be to **Jump In The Deep End** and it was important to hold her back. **All of our efforts work to ensure that our clients never have another anxiety attack once they begin therapy,** and few do when they follow our instructions closely. This is why we told Tina, specifically, not to do more than the same two blocks in homework that she had been practicing in therapy. Tina worked on this segment for two sessions **(Repetition**). Finally she could drive it at a Level 4. It was now time to move on to the next step.

The next three sessions were spent moving Tina three, four and then five blocks into traffic. We were still working during a time-of-day when traffic was not as heavy. After ten sessions Tina was beginning to see that it would not be long before she could drive comfortably any time. She was feeling this way because her general anxiety level was coming down. At this point, she was leaving her *"safety kit"* at home, and feeling much more confident about leaving the house without it. Tina also reported she was traveling as a passenger with comfort now, and said that her husband was amazed at how much "calmer" she was around the house. *"We can even go across town to his favorite restaurant,"* she happily told us.

It was now time for Tina to work on the *"feeder"* streets that circle the freeways. She wanted to know if she could go ahead and start on the freeways now **(Jumping In The Deep End)**? We informed her that her first task was to travel on the feeders **around** the freeways until she could do this comfortably **(Small Step By Small Step and Repetition)**. She discovered that because she had been *"in traffic"* already, that the traffic around the feeder was less anxiety-producing for her.

She made her first trip around the freeway at a Level 5. We worked for one entire session with Tina traveling the feeder streets (**Repetition and Small Step By Small Step).** She had only mild anxiety on the first day.

The second day Tina was ready to get on the freeway. She had lowered her general anxiety level by her **Small Step By Small Step** work and by doing her "**Choice Practice.**" She was no longer dreading attempting the freeway. We still wanted her to progress slowly. She also spoke to us about getting off her anti-depressant and her physician agreed to lower her medication. *"I'm no longer feeling depressed or as anxious and I don't think I need it."*

She began her first *"freeway session"* (with us following her) by getting on the freeway, traveling to the first exit and getting off (**Small Step By Small Step**) the freeway. She had an anxiety level of 6 the first time. She had a few physical symptoms, but they were manageable. Tina was ecstatic, she had not been on the freeway for two years, and she had driven on it without having an anxiety attack.

As we had done earlier in therapy on the busy streets, she mastered one exit at a time, first with us behind her and then without us **(Small Step By Small Step**). Occasionally, she would have a "*peak*" of anxiety and when that happened we would take a break. She would sit in her car and read a magazine **(Distraction**) until her anxiety came down to a workable level (5). She would then go back out and practice again **(Repetition**). **We would always follow her on the first trip of a new step and anytime she seemed to have a little more trouble than usual.**

It only took Tina nineteen sessions to master driving alone on the freeways again. By the end of treatment she was off her anti-depressants and no longer needed her "*safety kit.*" Tina did not have an anxiety attack while in field work treatment.

On a three-year follow up, Tina was still off medication and "safety kit" free. She had not had an anxiety attack since the night before her field work therapy began.

MARIA'S FIELD WORK

Maria was only having anxiety attacks when she tried to eat out, so she stopped going to restaurants three years ago. Since then she had slowly begun to have problems in other situations. This is a usual pattern for people who have anxiety attacks. Soon she was having trouble waiting in lines at department stores, grocery stores or any place she could not get out of quickly or easily. Her social life was severely restricted. She had unhappily discovered there is hardly a restaurant, movie, play, or sports event that did not involve standing in a line.

Because Maria's problem remained untreated for three years, her fear and general anxiety had escalated. Many areas she had not originally had problems with were now impossible for her to attempt.

In our first session with Maria, we explained that anxiety, particularly anxiety *attacks*, behaved similarly to *"weeds growing in a garden".* Left unattended, they would eventually spread over the entire yard as these anxiety attacks would take over many other areas of her life. **The fuel for this growth is *avoidance*.** With alarm, Maria had watched her disability grow. She admitted she had given up too much in her life in an attempt to *avoid* experiencing another anxiety attack, but she had no idea how her avoidance only insured that she would continue to have problems.

Like all of our clients, Maria had read many books on anxiety and had tried using *"positive thinking" and "affirmations"* to control her anxiety, but with little results. An intelligent person who persevered, Maria had worked on *"changing her thinking"* diligently. It was not from lack of effort that Maria was not better.

We explained that her anxiety level was much too high to have much success using *"positive thinking"* alone. What she needed was to start successfully approaching her areas of avoidance. By so doing, she could reduce her anxiety level and stop her catastrophic thinking. Maria was ready to feel and think differently. It had been three very long years since she had felt normal.

We arranged to meet at a local mall where there were many fast-food and take-out restaurants. We met at 2:00 p.m., when most of the lunch hour rush had gone. Maria reported her anxiety level was very high before she came to meet us, in fact she had badly wanted to call and cancel. We explained to her that the first session was usually the worst, only because she had no idea what we might ask her to do. But after the first session she would understand that she was in the *"drivers seat"* and that she would not have to do anything she didn't want to do.

She admitted this was the first time in a year she had even been in the food court section of a mall. She had avoided them because she never knew when she might run into someone she knew and they might unexpectedly want her to eat with them.

The first session started with Maria sitting in the dining section of the food court **(Small Step By Small Step) (Repetition).** She read our magazines and we talked until her level came down to a 5 **(Distraction).** Traffic was still heavy and although she wasn't going through a line herself, she stated that just watching the other patrons go through the restaurant lines made her anxious. So, we stayed in a very open area, close but distant from the restaurant lines **(Small Step By Small Step).**

In the second and third sessions we moved closer to the lines **(Small Step By Small Step)** until we were finally next to a fairly busy hamburger take-out. Every time we moved closer we would have Maria read until her level came down to normal. Occasionally (every thirty minutes) she could take a ten minute break and walk around the mall **(Distraction).** The breaks helped lower her anxiety level. Finally, Maria could sit next to the lines at the restaurants at a level of 4. We would usually repeat the exercise several times to make sure she was comfortable **(REPETITION).**

At this point we started giving Maria homework to practice between sessions. She was instructed to take late lunches and go to fast food restaurants near her work and sit and only read a magazine **(CHOICE PRACTICE).**

By the end of the third session we asked Maria to walk near a line where customers were waiting to order. She was to stand near the line but not in it **(SMALL STEP BY SMALL STEP).** She did this and reported she was at a Level 5, until someone walked up behind her who thought she was standing in line. She moved quickly away but she immediately thought, *"What if it was very crowded and I couldn't get out?"* It was time for Maria to sit and read **(DISTRACTION).** It took her fifteen minutes for her level to come down to a 4 again. Then she repeated the exercise **(REPETITION).** This time her level remained low when someone stood behind her. She was surprised she didn't get anxious and reported she felt a little more confident even after only three sessions.

During session four we had Maria stand in line, knowing that whenever her anxiety *"peaked"* she was to leave the line. This was still at a relatively busy time of day, so we always watched the traffic and didn't go to the busier food lines **(SMALL STEP BY SMALL STEP).** For homework, she was to wait until there was no one in line at the fast food restaurant and order one item.

In session five, Maria was feeling she could go through a busier food line, so we agreed *if* she promised to leave the line if she became anxious **(SMALL STEP BY SMALL STEP).** We reminded her not to **WHITE KNUCKLE.** As she walked up to get in line, two people came up behind her. But, she went through the line, ordered a coke, came back and happily reported her level never went above a 4. She was now ready to practice during a busier time of day.

The next session we agreed to meet at noon, in the same food court. Maria reported her anxiety level was higher today. The crowds were reminding her of times she had tried to force herself to stand in lines and had feelings of closeness and hyperventilation **(WHITE KNUCKLING).** Because we expected her initial anxiety to be higher, we immediately asked Maria to sit and read **(DISTRACTION).** After five minutes she told us that her level had gone down to a 5. We pointed out to her, that initially she was reading for twenty minutes before she could get her anxiety down. Lately, even in much more anxiety-producing situations, five minutes was all it would take to bring her level down again. She told us she had been taking her *"special magazine"* to work and was making herself take breaks and read and her anxiety level at work was much lower.

Maria's first task was to go through a short lunch line. She did this, and there was only one person behind her, so she felt only a little anxiety **(SMALL STEP BY SMALL STEP).** We wanted Maria to only go through a short line today because the food court was more crowded and noisier during this time of day **(SMALL STEP BY SMALL STEP).** Maria practiced several times going through the short line and buying only one item each time **(REPETITION).** She now required only short breaks of reading to get her level down **(DISTRACTION).** She was very pleased with her progress. This was the most crowded place she had been to in *three years* and she was *not* having anxiety attacks!

The next two sessions, Maria practiced waiting in longer lines **(SMALL STEP BY SMALL STEP)** and repeated going through the lines until she was comfortable **(REPETITION).** We suggested she take her magazine through the lines with her during these first few practices. Just in case her level went up, she would have some means of **DISTRACTION.** She took her magazine, but only had to look at it once. She was handling the noise and crowds well. She reported it felt better to have the magazine with her, even if she didn't read it.

The next exercise was for her to go through the line and buy lunch, *"without"* the magazine **(SMALL STEP BY SMALL STEP).** She smiled as she handed it over to us. *"I was becoming attached to that,"* she said. We smiled and replied, *"We noticed!* We did not want her to feel that she needed the magazine as a *"safety kit."* Then, Maria went through the line, bought her lunch, and reported her level never went over a 4.

We spent two more sessions with Maria. We held these two sessions at the cafeteria, were she had her first anxiety attack. Her anticipatory anxiety was a little higher the first day but quickly came down once she arrived. Maria waited until the line was short and went through and bought one item, at a Level 4 **(SMALL STEP BY SMALL STEP).** She then practiced going through longer lines buying one item with no problem (Level 4)

(REPETITION). We instructed her to practice this step for homework **(REPETITION).**

The last session Maria reported her homework went well, she had practiced without her *"safety magazine".* Maria's confidence was high and she practiced going through longer lines at a Level 4. After a one-year follow up, Maria said she was still enjoying her lunch breaks at the cafeteria. She also (now) looked forward to going out to different restaurants with her coworkers.

REVIEW

Most of our clients stay in therapy from three weeks to three months. By focusing on lowering their general anxiety level through small step approaching, their competency quickly forms and they're able to think clearly about their condition. They no longer feel confused and hopeless and their depression quickly disappears. What about the other problems in these clients lives? Surely having anxiety attacks leads to other problems in their family and marriage? This is true and these issues were also of concern to us.

Psychotherapy for these issues must still focus on avoidance behavior. Frequently they were also avoiding issues with a spouse, parent, coworker, boss, etc. It is important for them to understand how they over use *"quick fixing"* and *"avoidance"* in other areas in their life. Sometimes they would bring up BIG STEP or JUMP IN THE DEEP END issues like divorce or changing jobs. We remind them that they needed to complete their SMALL STEP work of learning to drive or shop alone before they approach these issues. Even if they had a profound problem - like living with an active alcoholic - their success came as quickly as those who lived in more normal surroundings. Although these issues were distracting and upsetting, they didn't need to resolve these other issues for this treatment to be successful and to feel less anxious. Often, after the person regains their self-confidence and independence through field work, the solution to other issues becomes quite clear . . . and attainable. The best way, according to our experience, to help them handle their problems is to teach them how to *"practically"* lower their anxiety, so they are not plagued with *"anxious thinking"* and the confusion it causes in every area of their life. Ask any highly anxious person and they will tell you, *"If I just wasn't so anxious I know I would approach many things in my life differently."* Field work can give this to them in a short period of time.

Chapter 8

INTIMIDATION AND ANXIETY

When an individual comes to us for treatment, we begin by evaluating what the person is *avoiding* in an effort to control their anxiety. We discover if they're not avoiding activities, they are usually avoiding a person who might be intimidating them (harassing, annoying, nagging, teasing). The intimidator can be a parent, a spouse, an ex-spouse, son, daughter, friend, boss, co-worker or client, anyone who is threatening to them on a continuous basis.

* * *

Ben had been having anxiety attacks off and on for several years. Ben was 6' 5" and weighed 230 pounds and was an unlikely candidate for intimidation. When asked about areas of avoidance, Ben reported he had started to avoid some sales calls because of his anxiety. However, his main problem turned out to be his ex-wife, Linda. Ben and Linda, two years prior, had gotten a divorce on grounds of incompatibility. Both wanted custody of their two children which was settled by the court. He lost primary custody, but received the usual every-other-weekend with the children. He was also required to pay monthly child support.

Ben told us that Linda would call his office several times a month for extra money *beyond* legal child support. Linda's calls were always to tell Ben how poorly the children were doing, and these calls always left him feeling guilty and worried about the children. Since his ex-wife had a good-paying job, he felt her repeated requests for extra money were unfair. But, he also felt obligated to help his children however he could.

Because her calls were emotionally upsetting, and Linda seemed relentless in her efforts to make him feel guilty, he started to avoid them. His secretary would take

Linda's messages and he would call her a few days later, usually with much anxiety. He also began to avoid checking his messages at work and tried to stay out of the office as much as possible.

* * *

Ben had a long history of avoiding conflict and letting others intimidate him. He related this uncomfortability-with-conflict to being scolded by his parents for fighting with a schoolmate when he was in the 2nd grade. Because Ben was large for his age, his parents did not allow him to fight with others, fearing he might seriously hurt them. This made a profound impact on Ben. This family rule *"de-clawed"* him and left him defenseless in dealing with *"schoolyard bullies."* This also led to more bullying, since many of those smaller than Ben, reveled in the fact that they could make someone Ben's size back down.

School had been an unhappy affair for Ben. When he was 15, he had his first anxiety attack at school. His early childhood restriction by his parents not to fight had severe consequences for him. In Ben's case he had no self-defense for dealing with "*schoolyard politics*" or for the inevitability of conflict with peers that life sometimes brings.

What could Ben do? Because of his size he could not easily hide. His parents didn't realize that learning how to deal with intimidating schoolmates is as important as the lessons taught in the school room. Ben's parents neglected to teach him about the important middle-ground between being a bully and *"cowing down*" to others.

When our son, Ian, was in the sixth grade, he told us he had befriended a boy in his school who was being picked on by other children. I asked him why the boy was being picked on. He explained to me in his own wisdom, that there are two types of kids, those who stand up for themselves, and those who don't. The other boy was the type who wouldn't stand up for himself, so other children would pick on him. This happens all too often in schools, and we've all witnessed this in one form or another.

This is one of those facts of life many people find unpleasant, and have trouble accepting. Though the human race has made many cultural progressions and technological advancements, many of our behaviors are tied to our primitive past. Many families, school groups, businesses, and other organizations operate on a similar *"pecking order"* found in the typical hen house.

Our definition of a *"pecking order"* is a basic social order in an organization where some people peck (harass, annoy, nag, tease) other people, but are not pecked on themselves. Here also, some people peck on others and are also pecked on, while still other people get pecked on but don't peck back. Many people who have anxiety attacks find they are at the bottom of this social order, the ones who gets pecked, but do not peck back. This is because they are often conflict *avoiders*.

As we have discussed in earlier chapters, when you *avoid* something or someone (an intimidator, personal conflict, a freeway, elevator, or a grocery store) your anxiety level escalates. Because intimidation is a cause of high levels of anxiety, lets look at some examples of people who are in relationships with intimidating people.

BOB AND HIS INTIMIDATING COWORKER

Bob, a computer engineer, had been recruited by a top firm in computer research and design. He had waited a long time for this opportunity.

He seemed to be getting along with all the members on his new team except one, Harold. Harold had been with the company for six years and although he was a *"peer,"* he would always correct Bob's research proposals in team meetings. A few criticisms were valid but, for the most part, they would focus on some small detail which stalled Bob's ideas on the drawing board.

Bob found, because of Harold's interventions, his ideas never made it to *"top management"* for review. One day, Bob decided he would invite Harold to lunch, hoping he was imagining Harold's hostility and they could resolve the problem. Bob asked Harold to lunch on three occasions. Each time, Harold coldly refused. Bob even tried being friendly and complimented Harold's work in staff meetings, but the problem continued.

As most humans, Bob tried to avoid conflict. Bob hated to confront Harold, who had a reputation for having a bad temper and making scenes to prove his point. But because of Harold's fault-finding remarks and attempts to put him down at these meetings, Bob began to worry about his job. It was six months since any of his ideas had gotten past the peer review and this field was very competitive. Bob worried that management would see him as a poor producer.

Bob began dreading team meetings; many of them he avoided. Sometimes Bob found himself reluctant to discuss joint projects with Harold, even when it was on a one-on-one basis. Harold seemed intent on making all Bob's comments and ideas appear weak and poorly substantiated.

In one particularly bad meeting, Harold seemed to be picking on him relentlessly. Bob began to feel dizzy and lightheaded. His hands trembled. He felt like the voices of the other group members were getting louder and louder. Bob saw black spots on the report in his hands and realized he might be close to passing out. He had to *"white knuckle"* the rest of the meeting.

He went home that night, determined to begin searching for another job. The physical feelings he had in the meetings were not worth it. He started to miss work on some days to avoid meeting with Harold. If only he could find a job *"without a Harold,"* but it seemed there was one in every office. Maybe he should consider going back to being a *"programmer,"* a position where he didn't have to be around so many people.

He had worked hard and felt he was good in research and design, but he felt he had no other option. Maybe he wasn't cut out for the competitiveness of design work.

MIRIAM AND HER INTIMIDATING MOTHER

Miriam came from a close-knit family. She, her two siblings, and their families all lived within a few miles of her mother. Her father had died when Miriam was ten, and her mother had never fully recovered from his death, twenty years ago. Her mother had not gone to work after her father died, even though the family doctor said it would be the best thing for her to do. She stayed at home and the family lived on a small pension and life insurance their father had left them.

Miriam was the oldest and although the whole family was close, it was Miriam her mother called on for help. When Miriam graduated from high school, she decided to move to a neighboring town. She had planned and saved her entire senior year for the move. A month before she graduated, she put a deposit down on an apartment in anticipation of moving in June. She was good planner and had saved enough money to live on until she could find a job. It was her goal to go to school part-time and become an elementary school teacher.

All of her plans were running smoothly, until, two weeks before she was to move, her mother became sick. Her mother insisted she could handle the house herself, but she became bedridden, and although there were other family members to help her, she seemed only satisfied with the way Miriam cared for her.

Miriam's mother urged her to go, but refused to eat unless it was something Miriam prepared for her. Miriam had a premonition that whether she decided to go or stay, this was a very important decision in her life. Hoping things would go well, she moved.

Miriam would go home on the weekends and see her mother but began to feel very guilty. Her mother was not eating well and was losing weight. When Miriam would start to leave, her mother would cry and tell her, her only reason for living would be to see Miriam on the next visit. Her mother's doctor said she was not eating well, but it was not "*life threatening,*" and felt Miriam should stay where she was.

After a few months of living on her own, Miriam began to consider her decision to move away from home a premature one. Maybe she should be home taking care of her mother. After three months she decided to move home.

Instantly, her mother began eating again and life went back to normal. For several months afterward, Miriam had talked about moving out again. Whenever she would bring it up, within a day or so her mother would again become ill.

When Miriam married, six years later, her mother insisted they move into a house close to where she lived. She said she wanted to "*help*" Miriam when she and her new husband had children. After the marriage it seemed she spent more time talking with her mother than before she got married and moved out.

Her mother would start calling early in the morning just to check and see "*If everyone and everything was O.K.*" After a few years of her mother's frequent daily calls, Miriam began feeling "*uncomfortable*" anticipating her mother's phone call. She always seemed to talk about how bad she was feeling that day, or what the doctor had told her to be careful about. Miriam had two small children now and was busy, and often didn't have the time to talk.

On mornings, when her mother would call three or four times, Miriam would get far behind on her family chores, but she felt too guilty to tell her mother she couldn't stay on the phone. The last time she had tried to limit her phone calls, her mother had acted hurt and said she "*didn't mean to be a burden . . .*"

but, continued to talk!

By the time Miriam would succeed in ending the conversation with her mother, she would be feeling hot and nauseous. Why couldn't her mother understand she had two small children to take care of, and a list of errands that never seemed to get done?

Finally, Miriam decided she would get an answering machine. This would enable her to return the calls when she had the time. The first day her mother called ten times and left ten messages. When Miriam was at home and didn't feel like answering the telephone, it would ring every ten minutes until she *would* answer it.

After a few weeks of this, Miriam started to hyperventilate and feel dizzy every time the phone would ring. She could not seem to make her mother understand she could not be *"as available"* to her as she once had been. No matter how she said it, she always felt guilty. And her mother continued to call.

Soon, Miriam found herself staying away from the house to avoid her mother's phone calls, and feeling more anxious every day.

* * *

JANE AND HER INTIMIDATING STEP SON

Jane married Tom after being divorced for five years from her first husband. Tom had been married before and had three grown children. Nathan, his youngest son, was now living with Tom and Jane. Two of his older sons lived in other cities.

After learning that his father and his stepmother would be moving into a new four-bedroom house, Nathan wanted to move in *"to renew"* his relationship with his father. He was twenty at this time and he and his dad had a tumultuous relationship for many years when he had lived with his mother.

Dropping out of school at sixteen, Nathan had not been

interested in working on his G.E.D. and actually had done very little since leaving school other than play his guitar and spend time with his friends. Being a headstrong child, his mother had stopped trying to influence him long ago. She had been unable to persuade him to go to work, so she encouraged Nathan to go and live with his dad. Privately, she hoped his father could help him where she had failed. Tom agreed to let Nathan stay until he could get a job and save some money for his own apartment.

Nathan moved in soon after his dad's remarriage. When Tom and Jane returned from their honeymoon, they came home to a party-wrecked house and found Nathan lounging on the sofa drinking a beer, his friends occupying various other seats, the floor, and three of the four bedrooms.

Within a few weeks, Jane began to realize her married life was going to be much different than she had anticipated. The basic plan for Nathan living with them was for Nathan to be working and paying a small amount for his rent and food. Nathan claimed he had looked for a job for six weeks and had no luck. The truth was, Nathan restricted his job-search to asking his friends if they knew any places that were hiring. He had not been on any interviews nor had he put in one job application.

Finally, Tom found Nathan a job at a local convenience store. Nathan kept the job for one week but was fired for being late every day. Jane watched as her stepson continued to lay around the house, watch T.V. and eat. When she asked Nathan to help with anything, he would tell her he would, but never followed through. After several weeks, Jane asked for a *"family conference"* to discuss her feelings about household responsibilities.

Nathan was pleasant and cooperative and said he didn't know Jane was feeling frustrated and overwhelmed by his behavior. He told them he'd try harder, but in the following weeks his behavior didn't change. Jane tried to be understanding of Nathan. She realized he came from a broken home, but he also ignored her authority and the rules he had agreed to. To add to that, she found money missing from her purse. She questioned Nathan about the money, but all he did was refuse to answer and stare at her defiantly.

Tom, a policeman, seemed not to understand what was happening in his own home. Jane began to feel it was not her house, but Nathan's. She began to feel uncomfortable with Nathan's defiant attitude, particularly when she was at home alone with him. He appeared to know he made her ill-at-ease and always seemed to do the opposite of what she asked him to do. She talked with Tom about her feelings, but Nathan was at his best behavior when Tom was around.

Jane began to think maybe she was imagining Nathan's hostility. One day after she had asked Nathan three times to wash the dishes he and his friends had left from the night before, she began to feel lightheaded. When she went into the kitchen to prepare dinner, the dishes were still in the sink and Nathan was watching television. Jane felt faint, and disoriented as she stood in the kitchen.

Jane decided to take a short walk, maybe some fresh air would help her clear her head. As she walked, she began to feel she didn't want to go back to the house. It was only an hour before her husband would be home and maybe they could go out to eat.

In the coming weeks she found herself more and more anxious about dealing with Nathan. Whenever they were alone at home, she would mostly stay in her room to avoid coming in contact with him. Her husband didn't seem to understand; he thought he was building the "*important bond*" that he had missed building with his son when Nathan was young. So Jane felt totally on her own in dealing with Nathan, and didn't see any way that she could change his behavior.

To relieve her anxiety, Jane decided to do volunteer work that would enable her to be away from home, and away from Nathan. By now, every time she thought about her home situation, her heart would start to race, her mouth would become dry, and she felt dizzy and overwhelmed.

* * *

HANDLING SCHOOLYARD POLITICS

Bob, Miriam, and Jane were all dealing with intimidators. They, like Ben, are having a difficult time learning some long-overdue lessons in "*schoolyard politics.*" Each of these individuals were in relationships in which their assumptions about how people should behave and respond, did not work. They were all frustrated that their attempts to deal in a straightforward manner and share their feelings and needs did not affect the intimidators behavior. Their frustration in dealing with their intimidator led to avoidance and increased anxiety.

An intimidator usually knows how their behavior makes you feel:

To confide in an intimidator your feelings of hurt, sadness or frustration often makes the situation worse. They might say they understand what you're feeling but it still doesn't change their behavior. This lack of responsiveness does not necessarily make them "*bad*" people. It usually means their anxiety level is high and they have learned some very "*different techniques*" than you for avoiding or "*quick fixing*" their anxiety.

You see, where some people learn to "accommodate" or "understand" everyone to avoid the anxiety of conflict, some people avoid being placed in an accommodating role. Intimidation is their way of not letting others make them anxious. They are particularly interested in getting you to accommodate their anxiety. Any of their anxiety they can get someone else to "take on" is a little less they will have to deal with.

Bob's co-worker, Harold, was an anxious person. The appearance of a new employee (one with high qualifications) made his own anxiety escalate. Harold's technique for dealing with this new threat was to "peck" Bob out of the social order, which he was successful in doing. It didn't take long for Bob to start looking for another job.

However, it was Bob's responsibility to stop Harold from passing his "anxious overflow" onto him. Bob cannot change Harold from being an intimidator (or an anxious person), but he can stop Harold from "pecking" on him.

"Life" will keep giving you the same problem until you solve it:

Until you learn how to deal with intimidation, you will find it re-occurring wherever you go. Accommodating Harold's behavior or moving to a new job is not the answer. Bob later realized that he had to learn to deal with the "Harold's" of this world because they're everywhere.

Bob's co-worker, Harold, intimidated him for over a year. He was relieved when Harold was transferred to a different regional office. Bob was just starting to enjoy his job again when his boss was promoted and the intimidator was transferred back to become Bob's boss. As Bob discovered, avoidance only leads to bigger problems later. **Unfortunately, intimidators will always find accommodators . . . to help them manage their anxiety level.**

Most accommodators see problems as black or white. In this case, to either fight or take flight. Both have consequences in dealing with family, schoolmates and office staff. To physically come to blows can result in injury and sometimes criminal charges. To always take flight results in unhealthy stress and anxiety.

Many people choose to flee from conflict. They avoid intimidating people when they can or they become overly accommodating when they can't. The best way to deal with an intimidating person is the way most animals deal with this problem, through *"symbolic communication."* Since fighting can result in physical injury and threaten survival, most animals instinctively deal with dominance or status issues through "symbolic communication".

The most powerful way to communicate status or power is with your eyes. **Most anxious people avoid eye contact with people, especially with those who intimidate them.** Avoidance of eye contact has the same consequences as avoiding driving, shopping or riding elevators. It increases anxiety and lowers your self-confidence. Avoidance of eye contact with an intimidator is a quick-fix that will solve your immediate anxiety, but will eventually make the problem worse. **Practicing eye contact (not staring) is a very important step to take in dealing with intimidation.**

First, practice eye contact during the day on everyone. Get comfortable making eye contact with others. Then start practicing looking at the intimidator when you pass them. After you become comfortable with this step, practice looking and not smiling (but not frowning) at the intimidator. Smiling at an intimidator is often interpreted as "*appeasement*" behavior of a less dominant person. Once you become comfortable just looking and not smiling at the intimidator, practice it also while talking to them. By practicing eye contact and not smiling you will quickly communicate in a language that the intimidator will understand. This is because intimidators often cue on avoidance of eye contact and "appeasement" behavior in knowing which people they can continue to "peck" on.

Avoidance of intimidators results in a loss of mobility and status:

If the intimidator is a family member or co-worker, to avoid them means staying in your room or office, or avoiding your home or office. To avoid an intimidating neighbor you have to stay inside your house and not work in your yard. To avoid an intimidating friend results in not answering your phone or door.

This adds to your emotional stress and keeps your anxiety level elevated.

Intimidators are only trying to get their needs met, **but at your expense**, by passing their anxiety on to you. Let them be accountable for their own anxiety. You can't take care of their anxiety and yours too.

Jane's stepson was also an anxious person. So far in his life he had managed to avoid all of life's anxiety-producing challenges for young people . . . graduating from school, leaving home, getting a first job. And if he could successfully intimidate Jane into not making waves, he could avoid those challenges a little longer. However, it was Jane's house he was living in and Jane's life he was upsetting. It was Jane's responsibility not to let Nathan keep her away from her own home.

Accommodators are "Anxiety Absorbers"

There are many anxious people who handle their anxiety by "dumping it on others." Yelling, being emotionally volatile, inconsiderate or rude, are often signs of high anxiety in individuals. To be "accommodating," or too understanding of such behavior, makes one a dumping ground for someone else's anxiety.

Accommodators usually have several people who are constantly calling them with their problems. By the end of the conversation the person who called is feeling better and the accommodator is feeling overwhelmed. Accommodators try to "quick fix" others problems and anxieties. An accommodators intentions may be good, but they usually end up absorbing the other person's anxiety. Unlike intimidators they can't stand to see anyone uncomfortable or anxious.

There is a price for accommodators to pay for not setting limits. Miriam's mother was an anxious person, also. Having never dealt with the anxiety of being alone, she made sure she never would, by keeping her daughter close both physically and emotionally. Miriam's mother was "quick fixing" her own anxiety by leaning on her daughter.

However, it was *Miriam* who accommodated her mother's anxiety at the expense of her own goals in life. Miriam's other expense was, by accommodating her mother, she carried not only her anxiety, but also her mother's anxiety. Miriam, by not setting a reasonable limit on how much of her mother's anxiety she could absorb, **paid the price of anxiety attacks.**

Chapter 9

ANXIOUS THINKING

A major discomfort for highly anxious people, is that anxiety has a profoundly distressing and painful effect on their thinking. High levels of anxiety interferes with one's ability to remain objective about their problem. The more anxious your thinking, the more inclined you are to use avoidance to "quick fix" the pain. Anxious thinking doesn't create anxiety but it does greatly hinder your ability to constructively solve your problem.

Most anxious people believe it is their thinking that is causing their problem. If they could just *"change their negative thoughts and be more positive"* they would be less anxious and not have anxiety attacks. Many self-help books encourage this belief by proposing that one can lower their anxiety through positive thinking. In our treatment of people with anxiety attacks we have found this to be both a *misleading and an unproductive approach.*

Focusing on eliminating negative or catastrophic thinking when one is highly anxious is much like the man who loses his keys in a dark alley, but searches for them under the lamppost because there is more light there. Because of the strength, rigidity and consistency of negative thoughts, they become prime suspects for being the cause of one's problems. However, although negative thoughts restrict our ability to solve our problems, they do not *create* anxiety. **By *reducing* anxiety, the strength and pain of these negative thoughts evaporate.**

Our Emotional Brain

One way of understanding anxious thinking is to understand how our brain functions. P.D. MacLean *(Emotions: Their Parameters and Measurements, 1975)* has described our brain as a *"triune"* brain, one composed of three different brains, each controlling three different functions for us. MacLean defined these three brains as the Reptile brain (*the center core of the brain, including the basal ganglia),* Palaeomammalian brain *(intermediate layer of the brain, including the limbic system),* and the Neomammalian Brain *(outer layer of the brain, including neocortex and its associate brain stem structures).*

The Reptile brain is our "emotional brain" which regulates our physiological and psychological needs. The Palaeomammalian brain is our "feeling brain" which gives us an awareness of our emotions. And the Neomannalian brain is our "thinking brain" that interprets our feelings and develops methods for supplying our needs. In man, these three brains intermesh and function together as a whole.

The "emotional brain" is our primary brain since it is responsible for regulating our basic physiological and psychological functions. The "feeling brain" and the "thinking brain" basically provide specialized support services that increase the effectiveness of the emotional brain.

MacLean calls the "emotional brain" the Reptile brain since reptiles have developed this part of the brain but have not developed the "feeling brain" nor the "thinking brain". Mammals have developed both the "emotional brain" and the "feeling brain", but have not developed the "thinking brain". Man possess all three brains.

This is to say that reptiles react emotionally but do not have an awareness of feelings such as fear, sadness, anger, happiness or love as do mammals and humans. While mammals have an awareness of emotions they do not have a natural capacity for interpreting these feelings nor can they do complex problem solving.

Again, the "emotional brain" is our central brain in that it regulates our basis physiological and psychological needs. It also regulates our basic survival behavior of obtaining food, reproduction, flight or fight behavior, child rearing, establishing and protecting territory and social status. **The emotional brain has a predisposition for routine and ritualistic behavior and**

prefers stable and secure environments. It reacts negatively to major environmental changes or threats such as a job change or conflicts with a co-worker. These types of changes or threats create emotional stress since they frustrate the "emotional brain" in its attempt to regulate stability or security.

Our "emotional brain's" regulatory functions work much like the thermostat in your home's heating and cooling system. Let's say the temperature outside is 90 degrees and your thermostat is set at a normal setting of 72 degrees. When the temperature in the house gets over 72 degrees, the thermostat turns *on* the air conditioner. The air conditioner then remains on until the temperature drops back below 72 degrees. The thermostat then turns *off* the air conditioner. Through the process of turning *on* and then *off* the air conditioner, the thermostat keeps the house temperature around 72 degrees.

Many of our physiological and psychological needs are regulated by our *"emotional brain"* in this same manner. When our blood sugar falls below our normal level, our "emotional brain" turns on many physiologic functions to get the blood sugar back up to its normal level. Our "feeling brain" becomes aware of changes in the stomach, which our "thinking brain" interprets as hunger. The "thinking brain" then starts wondering about what is in the refrigerator. If you are driving in a car when you feel hungry, you begin to notice billboards with food advertisements. In this situation, as with most situations, what the "feeling brain" *feels* and the "thinking brain" *thinks,* is determined by the "emotional brain".

These same homeostatic principles regulate our psychological needs. If a loved one is too clinging, one's psychological need for *"space"* is activated. We start feeling overwhelmed or irritated and begin to psychologically distance ourselves by "tuning out" the other person, or encourage the loved one to become more independent. When they begin to get *too* independent, our need for "belonging" is activated. We feel lonely and began to take more interest in them. Again, what we feel and think is determined by our *"emotional brain"* trying to regulate our psychological needs.

Going back to our home heating/cooling system, lets say the temperature outside is up to an extreme temperature of 110 degrees. A normal air conditioner running constantly at full capacity under these conditions will not be able to get the temperature down below 85 or 90 degrees. By not being able to get the temperature down to 72 degrees, the system is not able to shut off. Operating for any length of time under these conditions will put a major strain on the air conditioner. In the same manner, when one's "emotional brain" has difficulties regulating our needs, "emotional stress" is created.

When the stress is related to an unstable and insecure environment caused by constant change, such as job changes, moving, financial problems, family problems, or conflictive relationships, one feels anxious and thinking become more subjective and catastrophic.

Anxious thinking is a result of the stress the "emotional brain" is experiencing in its attempts to regulate one's need for stability or security. To deal directly with the "feeling brain" or "thinking brain" is usually ineffective since they are only indicators of the environmental stress the "emotional brain" is experiencing.

To reduce anxious thinking, one must reduce the stress the "emotional brain" is experiencing. **To deal effectively with this problem one must stabilize one's environment through active and direct behavior.** This places the anxious person in a dilemma. They need to actively approach what they are avoiding in order to make their environment more secure. But, as they approach these anxious situations, their immediate anxiety escalates. They then experience catastrophic thoughts about approaching the situation which results in avoidance behavior. **By avoiding, the immediate anxiety goes down, but their need for security is frustrated which will increase their general anxiety.**

Catastrophic Thinking

People have a balance of both positive thoughts and negative thoughts. At normal levels of anxiety these positive and negative thoughts flow freely through your mind. Your thoughts are like clouds in the sky, they come and go, and generally you don't pay too much attention to them. At higher anxiety levels, anxiety acts like a hook in the mind which "catches" negative thoughts. At moderate levels of anxiety the hook is small, and when a negative thought gets caught it is easy to get it unhooked and it floats away. The higher the anxiety level, the larger the hook becomes and the harder it is to get the negative thought unhooked.

If our anxiety level is at 6 when a negative thought gets caught, we can still get it unhooked by using rationalization and reassurance. At Level 7 or over, the anxiety hook is too big for rationalization and reassurance to unhook it. When our anxiety is this high we have to wait until the anxiety runs it's normal up and down course. When the anxiety returns to Level 6, rationalization and reassurance become useful again and we can unhook the thought.

Negative thoughts that get "hooked" by our anxiety become catastrophic because of the strength and intensity of the anxiety behind them. However, negative thoughts are not abnormal and are not a reflection of character or personality. As stated before, our thinking is homeostatic in structure and we have a balance of both positive and negative thoughts. For every positive thought we have a negative thought. It is our level of anxiety and not our personality that makes the difference in negative thoughts.

It is also important to understand that anxiety does not create more negative thoughts. Anxiety just gives us *more awareness of negative thoughts!* It's normal to think about not wanting to have a wreck while driving on a freeway, or to lock your doors at night. The problem is not negative thoughts, but anxiety. It is our *anxiety* that hooks our thoughts and distorts our perspective of these thoughts.

Pendulum Thinking

Anxious thinking also causes you to think in terms of what we call "*pendulum thinking,*" which is based on the belief that anxiety is caused by a lack of positive thinking or "will power." To get over anxiety one just has to "*be more positive and get out there and do it.*" A typical pendulum-thinking approach would be to wake up in the morning telling one's self, *"This fear is all in my head. I'm not going to give in to my fear and negative thinking. I'm going to be positive. There is nothing to be afraid of. I can do this with the right positive attitude. I'm going to get out there and . . ." (confront my boss, drive the freeway, shop at the mall, eat in a restaurant, etc.)* The person then "*jumps into the deep end*" of their fear.

What usually happens when you approach thinking in this way is similar to how a pendulum works. Imagine you have a pendulum and on one side of the pendulum you have 100% Negative Thinking and on the other side you have 100% Positive Thinking.

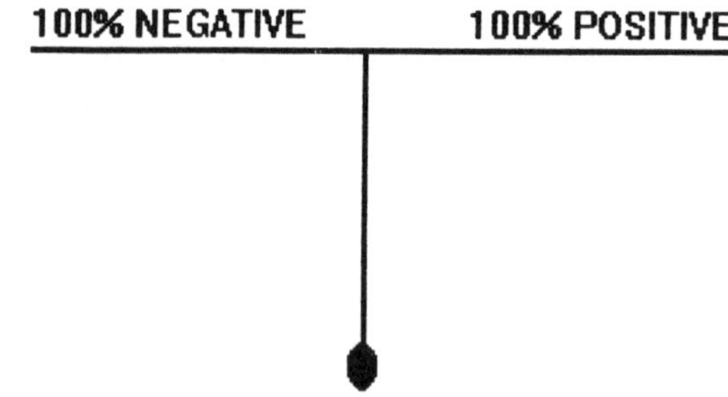

Now pull the pendulum all the way up to the 100% Positive Thinking side . . .

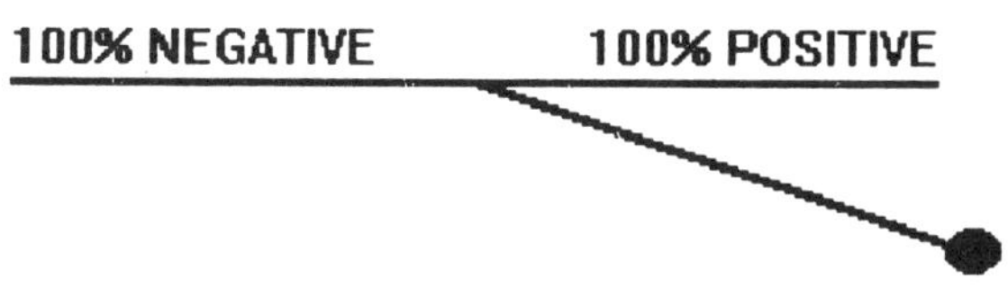

and let it go.

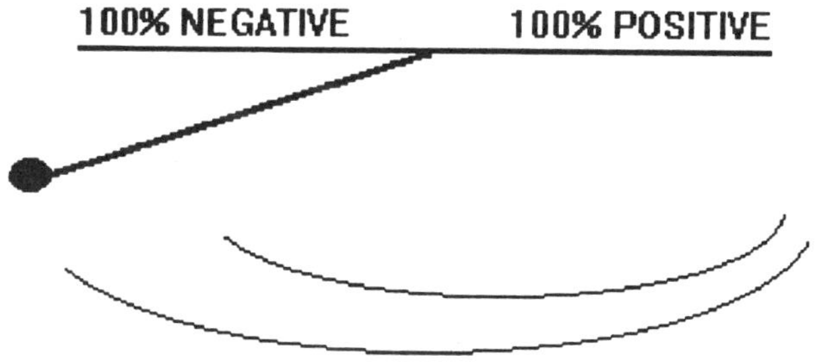

It swings back to the 100% Negative Thinking side.

The 100% Negative Thinking is what happens when you pump yourself up to face your fears and then *"jump into the deep end."* At the first sign of a problem with your anxiety (*your heart starts to race, your mouth gets dry, your hands start to sweat, or your mind goes blank),* you swing (*quickly*) back to negative thinking. *"I can't do this. I'll never get over this problem. I'm weak and no good. I'm different from others with this problem. There is something genetically wrong with me. I've got a problem that no one has discovered yet."*

This type of negative thinking is the result of pulling the pendulum too far to one side. 100% Positive Thinking quickly crumbles as soon as physical symptoms occur or negative thoughts enters the mind.

Realistic Thinking

Field work is based on a "***realistic thinking***" approach, which is both positive and negative, and realizes the difficulty of the task. "*This is a real fear for me. It is not based in logic but it does have a real component of pain associated with it. Trying to Jump Into the Deep End has not worked and is an overwhelming approach for me. I need to practice getting over this fear on a regular basis and in a step-by-step approach.*"

Realistic thinking will prevent you from a constantly "*jumping into the deep end*" approach to your problems. **Realistic thinking** also protects you from the positive and negative mood-swings that result from pendulum thinking. The intense mood-swings, as well as the resulting feelings of depression associated with high levels of anxiety, can be attributed to the pendulum thinking pattern.

Pendulum thinking is a form of anxious thinking you need to understand and be aware of. **However, it should rarely be a focus of therapy because this pattern will diminish as anxiety goes down.** It diminishes because it is a symptom of anxiety and not a personality trait.

Remember, changing your behavior of approaching or avoiding is the only real affecter of anxiety.

Chapter 10

THE DRAWBACKS OF OTHER TREATMENT MODELS

In this chapter, we will briefly go over the major theories and treatment models used to treat anxiety attacks. We have found these treatment models, although helpful for some, have only marginal results for most anxious people. Although these models are based on sound theory and scientific studies, and can be appropriate treatment for many psychological disorders, they have major drawbacks and shortcomings when applied to anxiety disorders such as anxiety attacks.

It is important to understand that medical and psychological theories are not *"absolutes,"* they are someone's idea or model about how things might work; they are tools for helping people. Society highly regards and widely uses tools that are good at fixing problems. As long as a tool is good at fixing a problem, people will use it. The reason we develop *new* tools is because someone looked closely at the performance of the old tool and decided it was not *"fixing"* the problem as well as needed.

This means that the assumptions used in making the *old tool* are not working. A new tool is then designed by using different assumptions that are more effective at fixing the problem. Since problems change and all tools can be improved, there is always a progression of newer and better tools.

One major problem in the field of psychology is when someone finds a useful tool, such as a hammer (*treatment method*) they want to *"hammer"* everything with it. Although a hammer is a useful tool for some problems, for other problems to be fixed properly, they may need a wrench, or pliers, or screw driver, or a combination of tools. For a tool, in this case a treatment method, to be of benefit to society, it must meet some basic requirements.

For instance, a tool that takes several years to fix a problem is not very useful, no matter how pretty or well-designed it may be. This also applies to expensive tools. A tool must also be able to *fix* a problem and not create other problems in the process.

For a tool to be useful to society it should:

(a) Fit the problem.
(b) Fix the problem.
(c) Show good results in a reasonable length of time.
(d) Be reasonably affordable.
(e) Not create other problems equal or worse than the original one.

Using these criteria, let's look at the tools used for treating anxiety attacks.

Medication: Do I have a "Brain Disease"?

The treatment model for anxiety disorders used by most physicians and psychiatrists, is the *"brain disease"* model. This model of treatment proposes that anxiety disorders are caused by a **chemical imbalance**, more specifically, an imbalance of *neurotransmitters* in the brain. Neurotransmitters are chemicals produced by brain cells *(neurons)*, which help carry messages within the brain.

When a brain cell is stimulated, it produces a neurotransmitter (**a chemical**). This chemical travels to another brain cell and stimulates it, which in turn causes it to stimulate another brain cell in the same manner. This operates much like how a telephone exchange network relays a phone call to the right destination. A healthy-functioning brain contains an appropriate amount of these chemical messengers. Problems begin when the neurotransmitters get out of balance and too many, or not enough of them, are produced.

What is presented to most highly anxious people by physicians and psychiatrists who use the *"brain disease"* model, is that the chemical imbalance is related to the genetic make up of their brain cells, that it is not the person's behavior or life stresses which cause the imbalance. Life stresses are viewed as bringing out the inherent weakness in the brain cells, but are not the primary cause of the imbalance of neurotransmitters. With the "brain disease" model, patients are frequently encouraged to reduce activities that produce stress. But, the major goal of treatment is to *"regulate"* the neurotransmitters.

Since this model assumes anxiety disorders to be caused by a biological problem *(chemical imbalance)* the simple solution is to find a medication *(chemical)* that *will* help the brain cells control the neurotransmitters. This is done by controlling the amount of neurotransmitters produced or absorbed, or by blocking them from stimulating brain cells. It is assumed that by reducing the over-stimulation of the brain, the person will calm down to a normal range of anxiety.

In the 1960's the benzodiazepines, Librium *(chlordiazepoxide)* and Valium *(diazepam)* came on the market. These medications *(tools)* were widely heralded, as were other medications during that time, as the solution to psychological disorders. By the mid-sixties, the problem of anxiety was assumed to have been solved.

Valium was being marketed as an almost perfect medication, in that it relieved anxiety with no significant side effects. This illusion lasted until the late '70's when it was found that more and more physicians were reporting depression as well as addiction in their patients on Valium.

Congressional studies conducted in 1979 on Valium and other *"benzodiazepines"* revealed two major problems with Valium; it caused *psychological and physical dependency* and had a sedation effect that *hampered* normal functioning. The medication was also found to accumulate in the body, causing the user to become increasingly more sluggish, drowsy, and forgetful.

Since the "*brain disease*" model for anxiety assumes that the brain is malfunctioning, the problem was again simple; find a medication that regulates neurotransmitters, is nonaddicting, and has no cumulative side effects. The result was *Xanax,* which was introduced in 1981.

Xanax was promoted as, *able to reduce anticipatory anxiety, would be completely eliminated from the body in less than twelve hours and was nonaddicting.* Thus far, this has not proven to be true (Consumer Report, Jan, 1993). People are finding Xanax to be as addicting as Valium and *more* difficult to discontinue usage. Many Xanax users are having more anxiety attacks after getting *off* the medication, than before they started using it! *(We have found this is caused by the person's "psychological dependency" on the medication.)*

Besides the "benzodiazepines", another group of medications for anxiety attacks are antidepressants (*Tricyclics, MAO Inhibitors*). These medications operate differently than anti-anxiety medications, but are still designed to control the neurotransmitters in the brain. There is an equal amount of studies that show antidepressants are effective in the treatment of anxiety disorders as there are that they are not effective in anxiety treatment.

One of the primary problems with antidepressants is that they produce many of the physical side effects that an anxious person associates with anxiety attacks. The physical side effects related to antidepressant usage are; dry mouth, dizziness, insomnia, becoming jittery and irritable. Often these side effects increase the anxious persons fears of having another anxiety attack.

Many people who have anxiety attacks are too anxious about the long term effects of medication to start taking antidepressants. Many of those who will take these medications, stop once they experience the types of side effects described.

Most anxiety sufferers end up developing a *"safety kit"* of these medications. A "safety kit" usually consists of several different types of tranquilizers, prescribed by different physicians. These are medications they keep on hand in case they have an anxiety attack, but seldom or never use.

Our findings in working with highly anxious clients, is that both the physician and patient credit results to medication that belong to *"avoidance"* behavior. The perception that medication is helpful in reducing anxiety attacks is often based on the anxious person's reports to the physician that they are experiencing fewer anxiety attacks.

What is minimized or, worse yet, *overlooked,* is that the anxious person is not sitting idly by waiting for their next anxiety attack to occur, they are busy making major changes in their life style. They are *avoiding* more and more activities where they experience anxiety, and are no longer going shopping, driving or eating in restaurants. They are developing "*safety people*" who they will not go anywhere without. In their attempt to control their anxiety attacks, their world is becoming smaller and more unsafe, and most find that medication does not stop this avoidance process.

When anxious people use medication as a treatment tool, they quickly develop rituals and magical thinking about it. Many anxious people on medication will have anxiety attacks if they leave home and find they don't have their medication with them, even if they've just taken it. They ritualize around the medication and will not go anywhere without it. This applies particularly to those mentioned earlier who have developed a "safety kit" of medication.

Those who *do* take medication have ritual times when they feel compelled to take it. If they can't, their anxiety quickly *escalates* until they do. Often, clients who are only taking a fraction of their dosage become frightened when they cannot take it exactly on time, and when they do take it, their anxiety decreases long before it is in their blood stream.

This type of medication usage is similar to the story of the man in New York, walking down a street beating a drum to keep tigers away. When someone tells him there are no tigers in New York, he boasts about how well the drum is working. In this same manner, medication is often given powers it just doesn't have. The anxious person is actually controlling their anxiety attacks with avoidance, rather than the medication.

By using our useful tool criteria, medication has three major drawbacks in the treatment of anxiety attacks. **(1)** ***Medication does not fit the problem.*** Most people who have anxiety attacks are too anxious about medication to remain on therapeutic doses. **(2)** ***It does not fix the problem!*** Present medications can only regulate the neurotransmitters, and are not able to change the basic structure of the brain cells, so treatment is one of long-term medication-maintenance. Most anxious people take the news that there is no cure as a lifelong sentence of disability. No matter how objectively or caring this is presented, it increases the patient's original fears of losing control, resulting in a further loss of self-confidence.
(3) ***Medication can create problems equal to the problem of anxiety attacks.*** Medication usually lead to a psychological dependency and sometimes a chemical dependency. It also creates physical symptoms that can cue anxiety attacks.

Psychodynamic Therapy: Do I Have A "Hidden Trauma"?

Another tool used for helping people with anxiety attacks is the *"hidden trauma"* theory. This model was first proposed by Freud and is much more complicated to explain than the biological model. It involves abstract and complex theories about the structure of the mind, how it develops, and how it protects itself from being overwhelmed by unwanted thoughts and feelings.

Freud proposed that neurotic anxiety, including anxiety attacks and phobias, is the result of an *Oedipal complex* (mental conflict) that results from unwanted childhood fantasies about one's parents, which the person is afraid to face. The person deals with these unwanted fantasies by repressing (hiding) them from awareness. *Anxiety* is the result of the person's insecure ego feeling threatened by these unwanted fantasies.

The threat is that these fantasies will unwillingly enter the person's awareness. When the person avoids recognizing and accepting these unwanted fantasies, their anxiety increases. Freud's solution to this problem was to slowly expose the person's insecure ego to these repressed fantasies by analytically interpreting the person's dreams and thoughts. Through slow exposure and integration, the person gradually develops enough ego-strength to accept and express the fantasies. This treatment method, in its pure and sophisticated form, is *psychoanalysis*.

The most common application of this treatment is "*psychodynamic therapy,*" a modified form of psychoanalysis where the therapist uses many of Freud's principles of ego dynamics but takes a more active role in the treatment.

Today, many psychotherapists do not agree with Freud's theory that all neurotic disorders stem from the Oedipal complex. Many theorize that neurotic disorders are the result of a person's excessive use of repression in dealing with their feelings of love, joy, anger and sadness. A more current trend in psychodynamic therapy is to view anxiety attacks, neurotic disorders and personality disorders, as the result of child abuse. Women with these disorders are assumed to have been sexually abused. The treatment for these psychodynamic problems is the same as with the oedipal complex; the person is slowly exposed to their repressed feelings or abuse until they have enough ego-strength to accept and express them.

Many therapists who use the "child abuse" model in treating anxiety attacks assume, without evidence, that the anxiety sufferer was abused as a child. If they don't remember the abuse, they are told it is because they are repressing the incident(s).

Many highly anxious people have spent long hours trying to discover the "*hidden*" abuse or trauma they are told is causing the pain and disruption in their lives. If they have anxiety attacks while driving, they try to remember being beaten or molested in a car, or they search their memory for a car wreck they don't remember, or speculate that their parent ran over someone while they were in the car, etc. Since it is not unusual in our society to be raised in a dysfunctional family, many anxious people will pursue this line of thinking even if it doesn't fit their childhood experience. They will anxiously and painstakingly search their memories trying to find clues of the abuse in order to resolve their trauma and find some relief from their anxiety.

This therapeutic model can create problems when used in treating anxiety attacks, particularly when there is no preliminary evidence that abuse has occurred. By assuming abuse before there is evidence, the therapist ignores that the anxious person is already experiencing catastrophic thinking and is highly suggestible to negative scenarios. To propose to an anxious person that they have experienced some mysterious abuse, probably sexual abuse, which they don't remember, only increases their anxiety. This is like telling the client "ghost stories" to relieve their anxiety. Anxiety sufferers can imagine and obsess about things that the therapist does not intend.

This is not to say that some people who have anxiety attacks have not had childhood traumas. Many have, and know they have, but to relive and express these traumas does not give them the promised relief. A major problem with this treatment models is it overlooks or minimizes the immediate avoidance behavior that is restricting the anxious persons lifestyle. Even after reliving and expressing traumatic abuse, the anxiety sufferers will still have to work with their avoidance behavior. Driving, shopping and socializing will still be anxiety producing for them.

We agree in principle, that traumas, thoughts, feelings or incidents that the anxious person is avoiding, will create more anxiety for them. Not talking about problems is like avoiding driving or shopping - avoidance increases and maintains anxiety. But, we *do not* agree that the anxiety reduction achieved by talking about avoided thoughts and feelings increases the person's ability to approach feared activities. Whereas, by first *reducing* their anxiety through small-step approaching of the feared activity, they are more able to talk about these avoided thoughts and feelings.

In using our useful tool criteria, psychodynamic treatment has two major drawbacks when applied to anxiety attacks. **(1)** ***It is not a good fit*** since the anxiety sufferer is usually too anxious to deal with and explore their overwhelming thoughts and feelings. All they feel is anxiety, and much of their thinking is catastrophic. It also takes a large *"leap of faith"* for the highly anxious person to expect that talking about their childhood will bring the amount of relief they are seeking. Psychodynamic therapy is, also by design, a *long-term* treatment and does not relieve the anxiety quickly enough to keep the anxious client motivated to continue. **(2)** ***It does not fix the problem.*** Even after accepting and expressing a trauma, the person will still avoid anxiety-producing activities.

Cognitive Therapy: Can I Think My Way Out Of Anxiety?

Today, the most recommended treatment for anxiety disorders is *Cognitive Therapy*. Cognitive therapy proposes that anxiety disorders are maintained by the anxious person's "false belief" system. (Aaron T. Beck, M.D. and Gary Emery, PhD, "Anxiety Disorder and Phobias" 1985) This false-belief system causes them to misinterpret their physical symptoms and/or external situations as more threatening than they actually are, which cause the individual to stay in a chronic state of alarm.

Cognitive therapy proposes that we all possess an *"emergency alarm"* system. This emergency alarm system *(with all its resulting physical symptoms such as racing heartbeat, trembling, or profuse sweating)* is a natural physiological survival mechanism. It readies us to deal with immediate dangers, such as coming across a tiger in the jungle, or an enemy in a combat zone.

In anxiety disorders, this "emergency alarm" system is set off by the anxious person evaluating non-dangerous situations as dangerous. Some people label normal physical symptoms as catastrophic (*"My heartbeat is irregular, I must be having a heart attack!"*). It is this chronic mis-evaluation of threat that keeps the individual in a constant state of emotional and physical distress.

Cognitive therapy claims to treat anxiety disorders by helping the anxious person understand it is their *"thinking patterns"* that sets off their "emergency alarm" system. The therapist first identifies the distortions the individual is using to mis-evaluate events or activities that have no real danger. The anxious person then practices identifying *how and when* they use these distortions.

For example, if the client believes they might "pass out" if they go into an elevator, the therapist then challenges this belief by asking if they had ever passed out before. If the answer is *"no"* the thought is identified as *"faulty"* reasoning.

Cognitive therapy believes, through the practice of identifying and understanding these thinking distortions, that the anxious person can become more aware and objective about these thoughts, and thus gain control of them. By *controlling their thinking,* they can prevent themselves from setting off their "emergency alarm" system and prevent anxiety attacks.

We disagree with the primary assumptions of cognitive therapy, that thought processes maintain anxiety. We have found that it is **avoidance behavior which maintains and increases anxiety, not the individual's thoughts.** Anxious thoughts are only *symptoms* of anxiety, as are sweaty hands and a palpitating heart, etc.

We have found that it is not necessary to deal directly with the anxious thinking, it clears up along with the other symptoms of anxiety as the person's anxiety decreases. To deal directly with the anxious person's thinking only postpones approaching areas of avoidance, and decreases their feelings of personal competency in the process.

We propose that anxious thinking is best used as a measure of the anxiety level rather than a cause of anxiety. The more catastrophic the thought, the smaller the approach step should be broken down. Again, we have found that it is much easier for a highly anxious person, *"to act their way into a new way of thinking, than to think their way into a new way of acting."* Since getting the highly anxious person to approach what they are avoiding is also the primary goal of cognitive therapy, we find therapy is more effective by *starting* with the *approach process*, rather than trying to deal with the thought distortion caused by anxiety.

We also want to make brief comments on two other treatment techniques used by cognitive therapist's; **systematic desensitization** and **flooding**.

Systematic Desensitization & Flooding

In **systematic desensitization**, the anxious person is first taught deep-muscle relaxation. Then, with the help of their therapist, they develop a hierarchy of anxiety-provoking situations according to their severity. The therapist then has them to imagine the *least* anxiety-provoking situation.

While imagining the situation, they are to practice deep-muscle relaxation. Once they can relax while imagining the situation, they move to the next situation in the hierarchy and repeat the procedure.

Cognitive therapy claims, that by learning to relax while working their way through the hierarchy, the anxious person will slowly change their faulty belief system and no longer fear approaching these situations. Again, we believe it is faster and more productive if the therapist works *directly* with the anxious person's avoidance behavior, rather than the thinking that accompanies the behavior.

Dealing with their *thoughts* only about the feared activity, does not effectively reduce their anxiety about actually approaching the situation. Also, in having an individual *think* about anxiety-producing activities, a therapist has no way of confirming what the anxious person is thinking about.

Since cognitive therapy assumes that anxiety is maintained by the individual's "belief system," it is helpful to assist the person in breaking down their "thinking processes," but does not help the person break down the actual *"approach process"* in the same manner. Usually, fieldwork by cognitive therapist's only includes one or two *"in vivo"* (confronting the real feared situation) sessions to prove to the client that their beliefs were false, that they can do the feared event even if they have to *"white knuckle"* through the session. Often, the relaxation skills developed in a therapist's office do not readily transfer to the fieldwork they must ultimately do in order for treatment to be successful.

Our experience is that the individual might *do* more, but will usually compensate by doubling up on medication or by developing "safety people" to do it with, and *still* avoid doing the activity alone. Since the cognitive therapist is not working in the field with the client, they are unaware of what safety devices are used. Overall, our experience is that it is much more effective for therapy to start by working *directly* with the avoided activity, rather than dividing the therapy into two parts, one part of dealing with the person's thinking processes, and a second part of dealing with the actual avoided situation.

Flooding, involves fully exposing the anxious person to the avoided activity and not allowing them to leave the situation. Although flooding deals directly with the avoidance behavior, it is still designed to challenge the person's belief system, not to desensitize them to the activity. Flooding proposes, that by over sensitizing the anxious person and not allowing them to leave, they will be cured of their fear.

The cure is the result of the client discovering that their belief that they will die, go crazy or faint, was false. What is overlooked in this process, is that it again *"sensitizes"* the person to the situation. They may learn that they can "white knuckle" through the activity and not die, but if they still have to force themselves through an unpleasant activity, they will still *avoid*, unless put in a *"have to"* situation. This still keeps their anxiety elevated.

Using the useful "tool" criteria on the cognitive model of treatment, we find it has one major drawback in treating anxiety attacks. **It only marginally "fixes" the problem since it is based on assumptions that do not fully address what increases and maintains anxiety (avoidance).** Although it deals more directly with avoidance, it primarily focuses on the *"thinking processes"*, rather than the *"avoidance behavior"* that maintains these processes. Because its primary focus is on changing anxious thinking, it only produces marginal results.

Review

In review, we want to again point out that the treatment models we have described in this chapter are very good tools for other treatment problems. Many people have problems that need medication, and many people have childhood traumas and repressed feelings in which psychodynamic therapy can be very helpful. All three of these treatment models can be helpful for people suffering from depression.

What we are proposing in this chapter, is that although these treatment tools are useful for other problems (like depression) they have major drawbacks when applied to anxiety.

Chapter 11

QUESTIONS AND ANSWERS

Q. You're saying that people should structure their field work so they won't experience another anxiety attack. I have been told and read in books that it is important to learn to *"accept" and "cope"* with anxiety attacks in order not be afraid of having them?

A. Many people have the idea that if you "white knuckle" through a situation enough you can eventually desensitize to it. We have found that this is **not** true! Suggesting that one can desensitize to anxiety attacks is like saying one can desensitize to burning themselves with a cigarette. No matter how many times you burn yourself, it will still hurt . There is also no need to learn to *accept and live* with anxiety attacks. The anxiety attacks should motivate you to take **action** to *lowering* your anxiety level in order to prevent them.

Q. If one follows your methods and reaches the point where they're not having anxiety attacks, then six months or a year later they have one, and they haven't learned to *"accept" and "cope"* with them, will this cause a relapse?

A. Again, it is a false notion that you can desensitize to anxiety attacks; the feelings are much too intense. No matter how much one learns to *accept* anxiety attacks, they are going to *avoid* activities where they occur. There is also no reason to learn to live with anxiety attacks, since there are many *practical* ways you can lower your anxiety level to a point that when you get anxious you don't "spill over."

People relapse because they have not learned skills in reducing anxiety, not because they haven't learned to "accept" and "cope" with anxiety attacks.

Q. Do you use *"flooding"* to help people overcome their phobias?

A. No! "Flooding" puts a person in a "white knuckling" situation. We have not found that a person is able to learn skills when they are placed in such a highly intense situation. "White Knuckling" keeps a person sensitized and increases their desire to *avoid* the situation or activity. They may learn that they won't die, go crazy or faint in a "flooding" situation, but they will still avoid activities they have to "white knuckle."

Q. What if someone is using medication for their anxiety attacks and wants to do field work, do you recommend they stop taking the medication?

A. No! When doing field work we recommend that you use all of your "safety" devices until you develop the confidence you need to let them go. It is important to keep your lifestyle stable and not make any major changes until you have developed confidence in performing the avoided activity.

Q. Does medication cure anxiety attacks?

A. No! Most studies show that a majority of anxiety attack patients relapse after they stop taking medication. If a person has not first, dealt directly with reducing their anxiety level it will still be at a "spill over" level when they get off their medication.

Q. Does relapse from getting off of medication indicate anxiety attacks result from a chemical imbalance in the brain?

A. We have found this not to be true. Many anxious people are hypersensitive to the side effects of medication which can cue their anxiety attacks. In most cases they are not really on a therapeutic dose of medication. Many only occasionally or rarely take their medication but they do keep it close as part of their "safety kits." To take away their "safety kit" has the same result as taking them off medication. To remove a safety devise without first *reducing anxiety,* usually causes anxiety attacks.

Q. Why is it that "positive thinking" does not work?

A. You can not *think* your way to lower levels of anxiety - it requires action. By practicing field work you develop skills in reducing anxiety. "Positive thinking," without a solid foundation of skills to hold it up, easily crumbles.

Q. Is group therapy or a support group helpful?

A. Support groups can be beneficial **IF** the group's primary focus is on *field work and avoidance rather than on the acceptance of their condition*. Group therapy that deals with intense emotional issues is often too overwhelming for people operating at high levels of anxiety.

Q. Do you recommend certain diets to help people control their anxiety attacks?

A. We have not found this to be necessary. Focusing on avoiding particular foods or over-emphasizing diets can get you off track in learning how to reduce your anxiety. It can also set up more avoidance patterns which will keep you anxious. We recommend a normal diet with all foods eaten in moderation. Remember food does not "cause" anxiety. If you feel anxious after eating certain foods it is more likely due to your general anxiety level being too high . . . high enough for you to begin to think catastrophically about whatever your doing (or eating).

Q. Does caffeine cause anxiety attacks?

A. Many people have developed "caffeine" phobias

because they've been told or have learned to associate caffeine with anxiety attacks the same way someone with a "driving" phobia associates freeways with anxiety attacks.

Caffeine phobias, like any food phobia, can become very intense with the person being obsessed with checking out every food product they buy or eat for traces of caffeine. Many will avoid eating food prepared by others because there might be caffeine in the food. "Caffeine" phobias usually begin because the person is at a "spill over" level of anxiety and is cueing on the physical symptoms (like shaky hands or heart palpitations) which caffeine can cause.

Q. Do anxiety attacks run in families?

A. Most anxious people come from anxious families. Families are both *emotional systems* as well as *cultural systems* which pass on norms of behavior and values from one generation to another. In some families, the members like to hug a lot. Whereas in other families the members never hug. Hugging is both emotional and cultural and runs in families, but is not genetic.

Much of how we learn values and behaviors from our families is like the story of the woman named Norma, who, when cooking a ham, would always cut off the end before she would bake it. One day her husband was watching her cook, and asked why she always cut off the end of the ham before she cooked it. She responded that she didn't know for sure, but that her mother had always cut off the end before she baked it, so she did also. She speculated that it helped the ham cook faster.

The next time Norma talked to her mother, she asked her why she cut off the end of a ham before she baked it. Her mother said, she didn't know, *her* mother had always done it so she did it automatically.

At Christmas, the entire family went to the grandmother's house for dinner and, sure enough, along with the other goodies, there was a large ham, **and,** the end was cut off. Norma, excited to be near the answer, asked her grandmother why she always cut the end off of her ham before cooking it.

"*I have a favorite baking pan,*" the grandmother replied, "that I've used since I was a girl, but it was always too small for the size of ham needed for our family. So, like my mom, **I would have to cut the end off to make it fit!**"

A simple story, we concur, but very true. Most of our behaviors, beliefs and methods of dealing with problems, we learned and/or picked up from our family in this same manner.

A FINAL NOTE

We hope you enjoyed and benefitted from what we've written. This book is not intended to be a "broad brush" criticism of practicing physicians, psychiatrists, psychologists, nor other psychotherapists, many of whom we both admire and respect. Nor do we want to criticize the health care community as a whole, because they do wonders for many.

However, through our years of working with those who suffer from anxiety, **we have found there is a major lack of understanding and flexibility in the health care community about anxiety and how it effects one physically and mentally.** Most people who suffer from anxiety attacks are being forced into treatment modalities that are more designed for the industry of health care rather than for the patient. Most physicians and psychiatrists are minimizing or denying the psychological problems that are created by giving their anxious patients medications. Most psychologists and psychotherapists are only willing to address those issues of the anxiety sufferer that they can deal with in the convenience of their office, even though an overwhelming amount of studies show that avoidance behavior is best treated with behavioral methods. (The Harvard/Brown Anxiety Disorder Research Program, January 1993)

Since most people who are suffering from anxiety attacks could have easily been prevented from developing disabling disorders if they had gotten early diagnosis and basic instructions not to avoid, **what the health care community does not know about anxiety is causing many people needless suffering and adds to the rising cost of health care.** Money that is generated through this ineffectiveness, in reality, diminishes us all.

INDEX

ABOUT THE AUTHORS

Cynthia M. Scott has a M.S. degree in Counseling Psychology from U. of Southern Mississippi. She is a Licensed psychotherapist with 15 years of clinical experience. Ms. Scott is the founder of the **Center for Phobias & Panic Attacks** and has been specializing in the treatment of anxiety attacks and phobias for over 10 years. She also conducts workshops for psychotherapists on the treatment of anxiety attacks and phobias.

Stan H. Looper has a B.S. degree in Psychology from the U. of Houston and a M.A. in Behavioral Sciences from the U. of Houston/CLC. He is a Licensed psychotherapist with 17 years of clinical experience treating Anxiety and Mood disorders.

Ms. Scott and Mr. Looper produced the video ***Gaining Control: Panic Attacks & Phobias*** for those suffering from panic attacks and phobias and for educating practitioners about phobias and appropriate treatment.

Ms. Scott and Mr. Looper are also co-founders of **Executive Speakers,** a management development program for overcoming the fear of public speaking.

They are married and have been practicing together for over five years. They make their home in Houston, Texas.

SELF- HELP TAPES FOR PHOBIAS

Cassette tapes by Stan H. Looper, M.A. & Cynthia M. Scott, M.S.:

***GAINING CONTROL OVER DRIVING PHOBIAS. . . . . #DP1. . .$9.95**

*** GAINING CONTROL OVER SHOPPING PHOBIAS. . . . . . #SP2. . .$9.95**

*** HOW TO DO FIELD WORK . . . . #FW3. . .$9.95**

*** HOW TO HANDLE INTIMIDATION. . . . . #HI4 . . .$9.95**

- -

Please send me the following tape(s): #DP1____, #SP2____,

#FW3____, #HI4____,

I am enclosing $ _________ (Please add $1.25 for one tape, and $ .25 for each additional tape to cover postage and handling.) Send check or money order (no COD's) to **Center for Phobias, 2100 Winrock, Suite 98, Houston, Texas 77057.** To order by phone call. . . **1 - 800 - 785-8855**

Visa ____, MC ____, AMEX ____, Card #__________________________

Cardholders Name____

Expiration Date ______________

Name ____

Address ____

City ________________________ State______________ Zip __________